CANADA: A Natural

Published in Association with the Royal Canadian Geographical Society

History

TIM FITZHARRIS
Photography and Captions

JOHN LIVINGSTON
Text

VIKING STUDIO BOOKS

Preceding Pages: One of Canada's most widespread carnivores, the coyote prefers hunting in grassy terrain. Its keen eyes and ears lead it to small rodents that it pounces on with stiff forelegs.

Mallard: A drake loafs on a floating log. The mallard is a "puddle duck", feeding by tipping tail-up to reach seeds, snails, and aquatic plants. Most puddle duck species are distinguished by a patch of bright colour (the mallard's is blue) on the trailing edge of the wing.

VIKING STUDIO BOOKS

Published by the Penguin Group
Penguin Books Canada Ltd, 2801 John Street, Markham, Ontario Canada L3R 1B4
Penguin Books, 27 Wrights Lane, London W8 5TZ, England
Viking Penguin Inc., 40 West 23rd Street, New York, New York, 10010, USA
Penguin Books Australia Ltd, Ringwood, Victoria, Australia
Penguin Books (NZ) Ltd, 182-190 Wairau Road, Auckland 10, New Zealand

Penguin Books Ltd, Registered Offices: Harmondsworth, Middlesex, England

First published in 1988

All Photographs copyright© Tim Fitzharris, 1988
Text copyright© Terrapin Press, 1988

CANADIAN CATALOGUING IN PUBLICATION DATA

Fitzharris, Tim, 1948—
Canada: a natural history

ISBN 0-670-82186-1

1. Natural history — Canada — Pictorial works
I. Livingston, John A., 1923— .II. Title.

QH106.F57   1988   508.71   C88-093007-1

Library of Congress Cataloguing in Publication Data
V82186-1   CANADA: A Natural History   88-50042

British Library Cataloguing in Publication Data Available

Printed and bound in Italy

Mossy Trunks: The trunks of poplar trees in Elk Island National Park are covered with mosses and lichens. Preferring moist, shady habitat these primitive plants grow on rocks, trees, and rotten wood.

Foreword

C anada's natural history is a complex and diverse blend of the land and its communities of plants and animals. Increasingly, we are realizing that the natural environment is not only fascinating and beautiful, but that its health is vital to our well-being. We are beginning to understand, as well, that we ourselves are part of nature and that we can flourish only when the natural systems flourish.

Who would deny the joy of hiking through a healthy forest, or hearing a flock of migrating geese overhead, or sighting a moose lifting a dripping muzzle from the shallows? Yet some of these joys are at risk today, because sometimes without thought, often from ignorance, we are damaging the world.

The more we understand the natural world around us, the more we will appreciate it, and the better we will act to nurture it, protect it, and live in harmony with it.

It is fitting, therefore, for the Royal Canadian Geographical Society to be associated with this volume, published on the occasion of our 60th anniversary. For the subject — the natural history of our land, here authoritatively described, explained, and beautifully illustrated — admirably complements the Society's objective of making Canada better known to Canadians and the world.

Alex. T. Davidson
President,
The Royal Canadian Geographical Society
Ottawa, Canada

Hawkweed: The flowerheads of hawkweed open each morning as light intensifies and close at day's end as shadows lengthen.

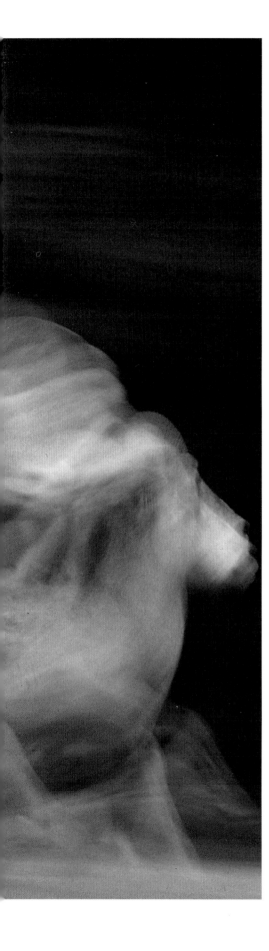

Contents

Bighorn Sheep: A herd of bighorn sheep race down a mountainside in Banff National Park. The males are armed with massive, curled horns which they use in ritual, head-smacking duels to determine dominance and access to ewes.

Golden Eagle: In a big cottonwood tree in the Milk River region of southern Alberta, a golden eagle feeds her downy offspring. These raptors prey on medium-sized mammals and birds — ground squirrels, hares, rabbits, grouse, pheasants, and waterfowl. Golden eagles mate for life with both sexes sharing the duties of nest building and feeding the young.

Introduction

I was curled up on the wood-slatted floor of the blind, waiting. The hours drifted by in the quiet heat of the prairie afternoon. Then just before dusk there was a soft thump. The impact vibrated through the limbs of the big cottonwood tree to my makeshift platform. I was instantly alert. The golden eagle had landed.

My eyes travelled up the tripod legs to the cameras and lenses that protruded from the nylon enclosure. They were aimed at the huge nest 10 metres away. Carefully I began to uncoil, raising myself little by little, until finally I could peer into one of the cameras.

Bathed in the sun's dying light, the great bird stood on the edge of the nest. She was exhausted from a long flight up the valley. Her heavy bill hung open, the tongue splayed out slick and pink as her breast heaved, pumping oxygen to thirsty lungs. Delicately shingled feathers, burnished gold about her neck and shoulders, were fluffed up to expose the skin to the cool air.

Suddenly, her head swivelled toward me. It stopped. The eyes — bleak, electric, lethal — locked onto the shiny faces of the lenses. I felt the tiny hairs on the back of my neck stand up. But her fierce eyes saw nothing amiss. The rectangular nylon blind and high-tech camera gear did not register on a brain that had evolved millions of years earlier. Soon her attention shifted back

11

to the still-warm jack rabbit gripped in her talons, and I knew it was safe to begin photographing.

As I watched, two eaglets rose like puffs of smoke from the tangle of sticks and twigs. They stretched up, swaying unsteadily as new muscles strove to support their oversized, downy heads. Only the taller one would be fed. The mother eagle ripped tiny bits of meat from the carcass and gently held them out for the larger eaglet. When it could hold no more, it preened luxuriously for a few seconds, and then attacked the smaller chick, driving it still hungry into a far corner of the nest.

Photographing golden eagles in the Milk River valley of southern Alberta in early April was the beginning of my last period of intensive work on the pictures for this book. Over the next seven months I would travel 60,000 kilometres and run more than 600 rolls of film through my cameras. My assignment was to make a pictorial record of Canada's natural history, be it of a tiny Ontario woodlot, an expanse of alpine tundra, or a coastal tide pool.

The more I saw of the country, the more I realized how much there remained to discover. And while I wanted to linger, to look a little closer, to see things a little clearer, Nature's cycle kept pressing me on to other regions. Later in April there would be the courtship displays of prairie ducks, grebes, and grouse to photograph. Then moose calves tottering on spindly legs would lure me eastward to the Lake of the Woods region. In the Bruce Peninsula soon after, wildflowers would be spreading their petals for a sun growing ever warmer as I began counting off the first days of May. By the middle of the month I would be in Canada's "deep south" peering at warblers along the brushy shores of Lake Erie and counting the number of crickets an eastern bluebird can pluck

from a dewy meadow. Afterwards there would be a more leisurely week or two photographing egg-laying turtles and singing bullfrogs in the marshes of the St. Lawrence River valley.

All too soon Gaspé and the Maritimes would beckon. Atlantic puffins would be hurrying to and from their nesting burrows, their outlandish bills stuffed with limp, silvery capelin. The red cliffs of Prince Edward Island would appear no brighter than in the sun-soaked days of late June, the time when humpback and minke whales begin to gather in the sheltered bays of Newfoundland. But as the whales spouted and waved their enormous, dripping flukes at my cameras, I would be spurred on by the realization that 5,000 kilometres away the alpine meadows of the Rockies were exploding with wildflowers, and that frost would soon ripen the Yukon tundra, daubing the sweeping, empty landscape with red and orange. So I would head west, and in the last days of summer I would hear the clacking echoes of bighorn rams bashing heads on steep slopes and watch salmon torpedoing up icy streams, dodging the paws of hungry bears. By October I would be on the Pacific coast in time for the first fitful downpours that would later grow steady and soak the rain forest throughout the dark winter. And just as I grew accustomed to the aroma of red cedar and sea air, Hudson Bay would lure me to its bleak arctic shore where polar bears wrestle in the snow waiting for the ice pack to form and carry them out to hunt for seals.

All this lay ahead of me as I sat in the cotton-wood tree listening to the exuberant songs of rock wrens and meadowlarks and, in rare moments, the whispering of air through an eagle's pinions.

While I chased forms and colours about the Canadian landscape, John Livingston would be on an exciting journey of his own, but most of it

Cottonwood Grove: Trees of any size are rare in the dry southern regions of Alberta and Saskatchewan except along streams and rivers. These cottonwoods, like other large trees, provide breeding habitat for birds of prey such as the golden eagle.

would take place at his retreat in southern Ontario in front of his typewriter. There he would set down in eloquent and forceful style his own appreciation of Canada's natural history. Roaming back through decades of experience and study, sifting through memories of countless discussions, of books written, of lectures given and issues debated, he would fashion a personal view of Canada's wildness. In this book his words would be joined with my photographs, each intended to balance and complement the other.

I worked at the eagle's nest for two more days. It was not easy watching the hopeless struggles of the smaller nestling. Through my powerful lenses, each cruel episode seemed to pass in slow-motion. Despite an apparent abundance, the smaller chick was never allowed by its sibling to take food from the mother. The larger eaglet would eat, preen briefly, and then attack. It hammered with sharp bill at the smaller chick, sending fluffs of down into the air. At times the starving eaglet fought fiercely, but at length it weakened, its breast becoming stained from seeping punctures. To this one-sided battle the mother always remained indifferent, her fierce eyes fixed on the horizon while the eaglets flailed at her feet.

Although I didn't know it at the time, this was to be the most poignant experience of my Canadian odyssey. The sprawling country's great drama of wilderness I had found in this nest — a small stage built of sticks, splashed with droppings, and littered with half-eaten carcasses aswirl with flies.

Climbing down from the tree for the last time, I heard something plop into the sagebrush. It was the little eaglet, driven finally from the nest. At last its short life was ended. It had seen the sun rise over the badlands, had snuggled against its mother's warm breast on frosty nights, and had spotted with keen eyes her regal silhouette flashing against the blue. For the eaglet, and for me, it had been enough.

Tim Fitzharris

LAND FORMS

The Lay of the Land

The entire career of *Homo sapiens* has taken place in a period so brief as to be invisible on the geological time scale. Long before our ancestors emerged, today's land forms were well in place. Even though as a species, we have experienced only a fleeting moment of the planet's history, we tend to see today's world as complete — as though the ages of mountain-building and flooding and upheaving were now concluded. We also tend to believe that geological phenomena occurred for the purpose of producing the landscape we see today. We often hear of the *final* retreat of the ice, or the *ultimate* form of the Rocky Mountains, or the *eventual* shape of the continents. This is a human conceit only. Volcanic eruptions and earthquakes, contemporary blips on the geological record, remind us that all is not over, and that earth processes continue.

In this first section we will focus on the Canadian landscape as we see it today and offer some of the major physical reasons why the lay of the land appears as it does. Overlying and often masking these physical

Long Beach: Low tide exposes barnacle covered rocks at Long Beach in Pacific Rim National Park on Vancouver Island. Although this stretch of shoreline is known for its sweeping, sandy beaches, most of the British Columbia coast is a broken jumble of rocky headlands and small offshore islands.

works are those of biological origin, and these are discussed in the subsequent chapters on Canada's life zones.

PACIFIC COAST

Only the thunderous hammer of Thor, it would seem, could possibly have crushed and fragmented the Pacific rim of Canada into the thousands of jagged pieces we know today. Surely no lesser force could have so tumbled, shattered, and rearranged the edge of a continent. The Norse god's legacy is a myriad of islands large and small, towering rockpiles of unimaginable mass, raging rivers plunging through precipitous canyons, as well as sheltered, sandy beaches and rich, estuary mudflats.

Today, instead of the might of the gods, we invoke the more ponderous theories of earth processes — vulcanism, continental drift, glaciation — to explain the origins and structure of Canada's landscape. However, it matters little which explanation we prefer; for the mountains, valleys, and islands of the Pacific coast existed long before our species emerged, and they are likely to be there long after we have ceased to look and wonder.

A satellite view of the convoluted shape of coastal British Columbia is one thing; a perspective from the sea is quite another. On a sunny day, snow-glistening mountain ranges form a backdrop for a great sloping and undulating forest of dark evergreens interrupted here and there by deep-cut gorges, river mouths, innumerable rocky coves and outcrops, and the silver foam of Pacific rollers crashing one upon the other without end. On a cloudy day — and there are many of them — the mountains are generally hidden. You will see swirling, grey sea, you may hear the muffled sound of breakers, and through the mist you can sense the sombre evergreens of the temperate rain forest massed silent and austere along the shore.

The climate of the entire coast is governed by air moving in from the Pacific Ocean. Whereas wild, seasonal swings of temperature are commonplace in the centre of the continent, here moderation prevails year round. Summer and winter differ markedly, though, in terms of cloud cover and rainfall. Along the southern coast, summers are noted for long periods of sunshine; winters tend to be overcast and very wet. Even in summer, however, cool air from the northwest is likely to keep the islands and coastal mainland north of Vancouver Island enveloped in cloud. In these regions the rainfall can be enormous —three metres annually is not uncommon on the outer coast of Vancouver Island. On some of the higher coastal slopes it can top five metres, five times

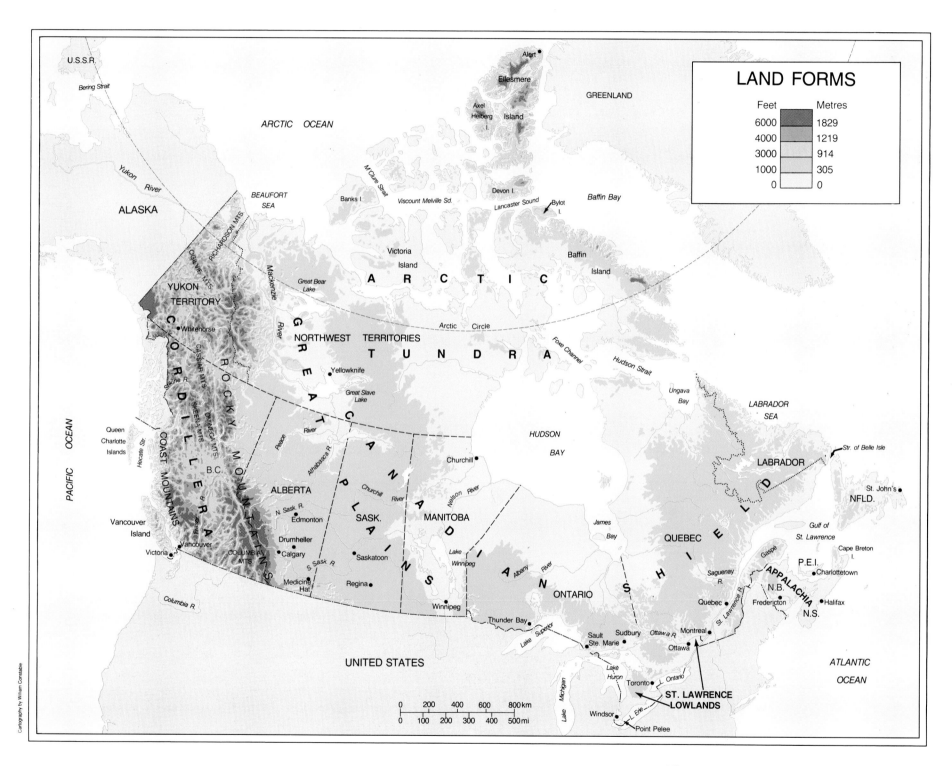

Montreal's average precipitation and ten times that of Winnipeg.

This precipitation is the result of the north-south orientation of the Coast Mountains, which places them in the path of warm, moist Pacific air. Forced upward by the mountain barrier, the air rises to cooler altitudes, and there its water vapour condenses and falls in staggering quantity. From the jumble of coastal mountains, a multitude of watercourses of various dimensions drains the rainfall and snowmelt into the Pacific.

But this is only a broad-brush picture. So topsy-turvy are the coastal land forms that depending on exposure, elevation (from sea level to over 4,000 metres), and latitude (1,600 kilometres from south to north), one place may be carpeted with ferns and another overlain by ice. Every turn in every stream bed, every valley, every slope is subtly different from the next. To know this land intimately would be the labour of several lifetimes.

CORDILLERA

Cordillera is the term used for the entire complex of western mountains extending from the Yukon south through Canada, the United States, and South America. The best known of these mountain chains is undoubtedly the Rockies, but it is only one of many in a complex mélange of peaks and valleys, trenches and plateaus that extends from the Pacific Ocean to the Alberta foothills.

It is a long roller coaster ride over a succession of ranges across British Columbia to the prairies: after the Coast Mountains are the Cascades, then the Columbia Mountains in the south with the Cassiar, Omineca, and Skeena ranges to the north, and finally the long stretch of the Rockies which give way to the Mackenzie Mountains in the Northwest Territories.

Coast Mountains: This huge range stretches almost the entire length of Canada's Pacific coast. Extensive ice fields, remnants of the last period of glaciation, are found throughout the highest regions of the Coast Mountains. The seaward slopes are generally fog bound, rain soaked, and thickly forested, and in many areas they plunge steeply into the ocean. Located just north of Vancouver, the twin peaks pictured are called "The Lions".

21

The Rockies are the youngest mountains in the Cordillera, as their toothed and jagged profiles suggest. Erosion has not yet had time to soften their outlines to the same extent as it has in the other ranges, most of which are about twice their age. As in the Coast Mountains there are many glaciers, which although impressive, are but vestigial remnants of the Ice Age. The Yukon continues the mountainous pattern of neighbouring British Columbia with the Ogilvie Mountains and Richardson Range extending to the Arctic Ocean, being the major formations.

When eastward-moving Pacific air reaches the Coast Mountains, it is relieved of much of its moisture, and torrential rains fall on the westward-facing slopes. The great windborne sponge is not completely wrung dry when it crosses the Coast Mountains, although the first squeeze is always the most productive. As it moves eastward, the air picks up some

Mount Rundle: The jagged contour of Mount Rundle rises above the town of Banff in the Rocky Mountains. The Rockies are part of the Cordillera, an extensive series of mountain ranges that stretches the length of North and South America. The Rocky Mountains are composed mostly of upthrust, bent, and broken sedimentary rock that has been sculpted by glaciers. Their contours are variable and include sawtooth ridges, towering pyramids, and blunt castle-like formations.

Ogilvie Mountains: Autumn comes early in the Yukon. In late August the rolling tundra is set afire by the scarlet leaves of kinnickinnick and huckleberry and the gold of dwarf willow and birch. At this time of year the Ogilvie Mountains, unmarred except for the thin line of the Dempster Highway snaking through the passes, offer one colourful vista after another.

replacement moisture by evaporation from lakes and transpiration from plants, so that each west-facing slope in succession receives rain, but generally in diminishing quantity.

This weather pattern produces denser forests on the westward slopes of the various mountain ranges than on their eastern sides. Even more dramatic is the dryness of some of the interior plateaus and valleys, one of the best known being the Okanagan Valley. This phenomenon, known as "the rain shadow effect," manifests itself in stretches of treeless grassland reminiscent of the southern prairies. These grasslands consist of narrow ribbons along the bottoms of steep-sided mountain valleys. In addition to the Okanagan and the connected Similkameen valleys, there is considerable prairie or parkland habitat in the interior valley of the Fraser River and its tributaries, especially the Thompson, Chilcotin, and Nicola. In some places the aridity approaches that of a desert. At Kamloops there is less than 250 millimetres of precipitation in some years.

As you travel through the mountain chains, there are so many irregularities and contours in the landscape, so many peaks and hollows, and so many variations in elevation that every turn presents a different arrangement of vegetation and topography. Within a few kilometres you can see desert, grassland, deciduous woods, mixed and coniferous woods, lakes and rivers, rockfalls and waterfalls, treeless tundra, and permanent ice.

GREAT PLAINS

One thing the Great Plains region is not, is perfectly flat. It is a series of treeless plains and lowlands, intersected by deep river gorges, and freckled with lakes, ponds, and sloughs. It is essentially a three-step structure consisting of, from west to east, the Alberta

Shortgrass Prairie: The driest parts of the Great Plains are in southern Alberta and Saskatchewan. This sparsely settled terrain south of Medicine Hat receives only enough rain to support shortgrass prairie vegetation.

25

high plains (ranching country), the Saskatchewan plains (cereal crops), and the Manitoba lowland (prime farmland in the south, with wetlands and woodlands in the north).

With the mountains as their western boundary and being relatively flat until the Ontario border more than 1,600 kilometres eastward, the Great Plains are wide open to continental air masses. Sub-tropical air can deliver heat from the Gulf of Mexico and the southwestern desert; polar air can make its way from the Arctic Ocean equally freely. Here the seasonal extremes of temperature are the greatest in Canada. In summer exceptionally warm air interacting with colder flows triggers severe thunderstorms, even tornadoes. The most devastating twisters were at Regina in 1912 and Edmonton in 1987.

Precipitation is generally light over the whole area. Because of the rain shadow cast by the western mountains, it is usually drier in Alberta than in Manitoba. The heart of the dry country is the South Saskatchewan River basin along the Alberta-Saskatchewan border. Having left most of their water in the Cordillera, the eastward-moving air masses gradually pick up warmth and moisture, and by the time they reach eastern Manitoba the rainfall has regained a level not substantially different from that of Ontario or Quebec. The rain which falls on the prairies tends to come early in the summer, thus serving grasses and cereal crops at the most critical time.

As one moves northward on the Great Plains, the prairie vegetation of the south is increasingly overtaken by aspen groves which in turn gradually transform into the vast coniferous vegetation of the boreal forest. The latter zone occupies three-quarters or more of the Great Plains, but it is the grasslands portion that has been most heavily settled and earned the most distinction.

In pre-farming days, the prairie ground cover consisted of grasses of many kinds, forbs (herbaceous non-grasses), scattered woody shrubs, and a few trees. The grasslands were kept open and free of trees by grazing and browsing animals, by fire, and by occasional drought. Generally fire is not damaging to grassland. It travels rapidly, it is not very hot, and it leaves turf roots intact. In the southern, drought-prone parts of the region, the ground cover, today infused with many introduced species, does not regenerate as quickly as did the original grasslands, but its adaptation to drought is nevertheless remarkable. Native grasses are extremely resilient to water deprivation. Their underground root systems can remain in a dormant state long after stalks and leaves have withered away. When the rains finally come, their recovery is little short of miraculous.

From a scenic point of view, the badlands are one of the most dramatic features of the region. Dry, windswept, and virtually without vegetation, badlands are found principally in the valleys of the Red Deer, Milk, Frenchman, and Big Muddy rivers. Here water and wind erosion have sculpted soft sandstones, shales, clays, and other sedimentary materials into a landscape of bizarre, contorted shapes. The heart of this arid zone is at Drumheller, famous for its fossil exposures now preserved in the Tyrrell Museum of Palaeontology.

CANADIAN SHIELD

If there is a single Canadian landscape stereotype, a universally shared mental picture, it is the forbidding, seemingly endless, dark evergreen mantle that stretches from the southern fringes of the arctic tundra to the Great Lakes and from the Yukon to Newfoundland. This is Canada's vast boreal forest of spruce, fir, tamarack, and pine, broken everywhere

Badlands: These strange rock formations are found in a few barren regions of southern Alberta. Badlands result when poorly cemented sandstones and other soft sedimentary rocks are eroded by rain and running water to produce intricate formations of mushroom shaped "hoodoos", winding channels, and steep gullies. Alberta's badlands are most extensive along the Red Deer River near Drumheller and in Dinosaur Provincial Park near Brooks.

27

with rock outcroppings and thousands of lakes. It roughly coincides with the exposed southern portion of the Canadian Shield, an immense expanse of undulating terrain which is Canada's most extensive land formation.

Above ground, the Shield extends from the southeastern tip of Labrador along the north shore of the St. Lawrence River almost to Kingston, Ontario. From there it angles north and west to Sault Ste. Marie, along the north shore of Lake Superior, west to Lake Winnipeg, then north again, bisecting Great Bear Lake, and up to the shore of the Arctic Ocean which it follows eastward, with long fingers extending north into the eastern arctic archipelago. From there, via Greenland, it descends again along the coast of Labrador. But that is just the exposed part. The entire Shield is a giant saucer extending to the Rocky Mountains in the west, almost to the Mexican border in the south, east to the Appalachian Mountains, and north through much of the central and western arctic.

Often described as the geological nucleus of North America, this colossal body of granite and gneiss contains rock that is 3.5 billion years old — three-quarters the age of the planet itself. The Shield has been relatively stable for a billion years, a solid bulwark that in a manner of speaking holds the continent together. Centred on Hudson Bay and Foxe Basin, the massive saucer extends outward in all directions, gently sloping upward. The slope is so gradual as to be barely noticeable. At extreme low tide along parts of the Hudson and James Bay coast, the mudflats extend as far as the eye can see.

In spite of the immense area covered by the Shield, its soils are remarkably similar throughout. There are obvious differences between the northernmost and southernmost regions, but they are due mainly to latitude, and the kinds of vegetation that climate permits. Canadian Shield soils are young and acidic. Young because the glaciers passed this way only yesterday in earth time; acidic because of extensive tracts of peat and conifers covering the region.

Virtually everything in this enormous area was influenced by glaciation. The drainage systems in particular changed dramatically as the ice front advanced and withdrew. When the ice sheet was greatest, drainage was mainly to the south toward the Missouri and the Mississippi rivers. Today much of the Shield drains to the north via the Mackenzie, and toward Hudson and James bays via a great number of rivers. Of course substantial drainage continues south into the St. Lawrence basin.

At its greatest reach, the ice sheet covered all of Canada south of Lancaster Sound and Baffin Bay, and east of the Rockies. Over most of Canada it reached its fullest extent about 18,000 years ago, levelling almost everything in its path. Nor was the withdrawal of ice smooth and uneventful. As the glacier retreated it stuttered, hesitated, and even reversed itself many times. At its farthest points of advance piles of rock rubble, called moraines, can be seen which mark a series of these hiccups in the process.

The most spectacular legacy of the recent ice sheet was Lake Agassiz, which endured for thousands of

Lodge Lake: The Canadian Shield extends over an immense area of central Canada. It is a relatively flat region of small lakes and evergreen forest. Lodge Lake is found west of Thunder Bay.

Sand River: Thousands of rivers and streams flow through the Canadian Shield, most of them emptying into Hudson Bay and the Great Lakes.

Rocky Tundra: The coastal area of Hudson Bay near Churchill is in many places strewn with rocks scoured by glaciers. Although unable to support plant life except for lichens, the rocks break the punishing arctic wind and in their lee hardy plants can take root. Hudson Bay is at the centre of the Canadian Shield, an enormous saucer-shaped land form that extends outward for hundreds of kilometres.

years in the centre of the continent.. The ice cap prevented the meltwater from draining north toward Hudson Bay and so Lake Agassiz was created. At one time it stretched from southwestern Ontario to North Dakota and Saskatchewan, including the southern half of Manitoba. As the ice slowly receded, the lake diminished, leaving at its centre the present large lakes of Manitoba and thousands of sloughs and pot-holes, as well as ground-up rock which eventually became some of the richest agricultural topsoil in the world.

ARCTIC LANDS

The first impression of the Arctic may well be one of lonely, inhospitable emptiness. But to those who love this land, it is ineffably beautiful, the crowning glory of the planet, an imperial diadem of ice all the more magnificent for its remoteness, all the more precious for its exquisitely tuned life processes.

All creatures who live in this singular, awe-inspiring region have been shaped by the primordial forces of ice, wind, sun, and the ponderous restlessness of time. They have been able to adjust their anatomy, their physiology, and their behaviour to extremes of feast and famine, and to relentless unpredictability.

This is a land of paradoxes, not the least of which concerns the water cycle. There is a great deal of water lying about in tundra ponds and tarns in summer, yet the annual precipitation is minimal, with less than 250 millimetres a year in most of the region. The most northerly islands are cold deserts with as little as 125 millimetres per year. Yet there are large tracts of soggy tundra caused by the slow rate of evaporation and the permafrost which prevents water from soaking into the ground. So the water remains through the summer, freezes solid for the winter, then reappears the next year augmented slightly by snow and rain.

From the air the arctic tundra may look smooth and soft, decorated with glinting ponds and sloughs. On the ground the reality is different. In many areas tussocks, hummocks, and frost boils make walking extremely difficult. In others frost-riven rock rubble reminds us of how little time there has been in these latitudes for the pulverizing effects of wind and rain and frost to produce even the semblance of soil. In the few sheltered spots, low birch and willow bushes do a little better than on open tundra, and although the process is agonizingly slow, their vegetative debris eventually breaks down and makes its modest contribution to soil formation.

In the eastern part of the high arctic it looks as if the Ice Age is still with us. Massive ice caps and glaciers cover many of the higher regions like they once did in southern Ontario 14,000 years ago. On Ellesmere, Axel Heiberg, Devon, Baffin, and Bylot islands splendid ice sheets flow from the mountains toward the sea. The proximity to Baffin Bay and the North Atlantic produces more snowfall than elsewhere in the arctic, providing the annual build-up that glaciers require to offset summer melt. At close range glaciers are not quite so beautiful. Like gargantuan bulldozers, their snouts root up enormous mounds of rubble — gravel, stones, boulders, and whatever else lies in their path — reminding us that far northern earthworks are still very much in the process of formation.

From the sea, the arctic islands provide scenery unduplicated on earth. Covered by glaciers and rubble slopes, with rolling hills here and there, and only occasional plant cover in the most favoured places, their sides plunge to the ice-strewn sea with frightening sheerness. Exposed rock faces are often striated,

with huge broken and shattered openings pouring meltwater into the frigid ocean. In striking contrast is the Yukon coast, which from a distance in summer can look most benign, protected from the sea by gravel-barrier beaches and from the continent to the south by the peaks of the Richardson Mountains.

ST. LAWRENCE LOWLANDS

There are cool fern gardens sequestered in dripping limestone caves on the Bruce Peninsula. There are sycamore and tulip trees along Lake Erie. There is Niagara Falls and the gentle, green plain of the St. Lawrence River. But these are only isolated features. The St. Lawrence lowlands region is known for one thing above all others: it is sugar maple country. It is the country set gloriously afire each fall in triumphal rejoicing for the season just concluded.

This region is contained on the north by the Canadian Shield and to the south by the Adirondack Mountains in the United States. It extends from the western end of Lake Superior to the eastern end of Lake Ontario, and northeast along the north shore of the St. Lawrence River to the gulf, but not including the Atlantic provinces. The region consists of two lowland plains, one on either side of a north-south axis near the eastern end of Lake Ontario.

As befits lowlands, which are the result of ancient flooding and sedimentation, these are generally flat or rolling, dotted here and there by heaps of glacial rubble and broken occasionally by aged escarpments. The best known of these is the impressive limestone and dolomite horseshoe of the Niagara Escarpment which runs from the Niagara gorge north through the Bruce Peninsula and then curves west across Manitoulin Island and into Wisconsin. The St. Lawrence lowlands are not solely a Canadian phenomenon, but stretch deep into the American midwest.

Buttermilk Hill: Aflame with sugar maples, a stretch of forested countryside near Sault St. Marie is a reminder of how the St. Lawrence lowlands looked before European settlement. Most of this relatively flat region has been converted to farms and urbanized areas.

Canada's southernmost mainland extremity is Point Pelee at the western end of Lake Erie. Like the larger Long Point peninsula to the east, this shifting spit of sand and gravel is continuously modified by wave action. Here are two places where we can watch land being shaped before our very eyes, not only year by year, but given a storm of sufficient intensity, day by day.

The climate is a consequence of both latitude and the presence of the Great Lakes. The weather along the St. Lawrence is more typical of the greater continental area, but in southern Ontario, nestled as it is among the lakes, it tends to be warmer throughout the year. Precipitation is fairly uniform in all seasons and droughts are rare. Winters are not as cold as elsewhere, but snow can be heavy in the lee of the lakes.

In the days before European settlement, a dense forest covered the St. Lawrence lowlands region. Along the St. Lawrence River and in more northerly areas, the forest was a mixture of coniferous and deciduous species. Southern Ontario soils are richer as a consequence of the original hardwood cover. From western Lake Ontario and along the north shore of Lake Erie the forests consisted in large measure of deciduous species commonly found in the eastern United States.

Yellow Pond Lily: A native water-lily, the cup-sized flowers of yellow pond lily are common in wetland habitats of the St. Lawrence lowlands.

Georgian Bay: Protected from the main portion of Lake Huron by the limestone spine of the Niagara Escarpment that forms the Bruce Peninsula, Georgian Bay is one of Canada's popular summer vacation spots. Its eastern shore cuts into the edge of the Canadian Shield forming many rocky coves and small islands. The opposite shore along the Bruce Peninsula is dotted with sandy beaches, caves, and exotic rock formations.

Although the St. Lawrence lowlands represent a small part of Canada, they contain unique features. Most notable are the Carolinian forests in extreme southern Ontario and a precious remnant of natural prairie that once stretched westward to the high plains and now is preserved in the city of Windsor.

ATLANTIC REGION

While the Pacific coastline appears to have been shattered with a sledge hammer, much of the Atlantic region looks as though it has been levelled with a steamroller. Although some hill country exists in Newfoundland, Cape Breton, and New Brunswick, most of the area is modestly undulating at best. Changing sea levels, tidal action, sedimentation, and glaciation have all contributed to the rather suppressed topography we see today, and they are also responsible for the multitude of delightful coves, bays, points, and bluffs along the strikingly varied coastlines of the Maritime provinces.

Newfoundland is a different matter altogether with its great rocks and massive cliff faces, its stony beaches, and its near-arctic demeanour. Much of its character derives from the annual arrival, via the Labrador Current, of icebergs. Silently drifting, slowly rotating and overturning, and ever melting, they appear offshore every spring. Even more impressive are the expanses of pack ice which move south each year, often to jam the Strait of Belle Isle, sometimes to fetch up on the shore, but eventually to disperse. These immense ice platforms, taking up hundreds of square kilometres, carry the harp seals which have been the subject of so much international debate over the years. They also carry the occasional polar bear that, for reasons of its own, has decided to ride the ice toward southern Canada.

The ice pack is strongly influenced by wind. Onshore winds compress it into thicker, rumpled

Bonne Bay: The east arm of Bonne Bay penetrates deeply into the rugged terrain of Newfoundland's Gros Morne National Park. This is a region of wild, uninhabited mountains, fresh water fiords walled in by towering cliffs, and oceanside sand dunes, caves, and volcanic sea stacks.

Percé Rock: Found off the tip of Quebec's Gaspé Peninsula, Percé Rock is an impressive monolith more than 500 metres long and 70 metres high. Once a part of the mainland, the rock's present isolation and shape is a product of the sea's erosive power, the most dramatic result being the famous "pierced" arch in its base. At low tide the rock can be reached on foot. Guarded by steep walls, the summit provides safe nesting and roosting for thousands of seabirds.

38

Blooming Point Spit: Prince Edward Island's north coast is an idyllic strip of beaches, sand dunes, lagoons, and spits. Warmed by the waters of the Gulf of St. Lawrence, the climate here is more moderate and less foggy than in neighbouring maritime provinces. The tiny island's landscape shows only remnants of the forest that once covered it.

masses, whereas offshore winds break it up. In years when the ice accumulates along the Atlantic coast of Newfoundland, it delays the arrival of spring sometimes as far away as Prince Edward Island and the northern shores of the other Atlantic provinces. Even without the ice, the water of the Labrador Current is so cold that it has a pronounced effect on temperatures along the coasts of Nova Scotia and Newfoundland.

Large bodies of water generally reduce extremes in temperature, making winters a little less cold, summers a little less warm. Oddly enough, Atlantic Canada does not have this typical maritime climate. The massive air streams generally arrive from the west, blowing in from the continental land mass where temperatures are more volatile, producing greater variation in temperature and humidity than is usual along a seacoast. Only a short distance inland climatic conditions are similar to those of the deep interior. On the other hand, the proximity of the sea can cause very localized climatic conditions. Weather forecasters in Atlantic Canada expect the unexpected.

Thanks to volcanic eruptions, sedimentation, glaciation, and flooding, soils of the region vary greatly from place to place. The vegetation tends to be boreal in the north (even sub-arctic in parts of Newfoundland) and in the south is similar to the coniferous-deciduous woodland of the St. Lawrence River valley and central Ontario.

Apart from the Newfoundland interior, much of the Atlantic region shows the effects of centuries of European settlement. In Prince Edward Island and Nova Scotia there remain little more than pockets of the boreal and mixed forests that once dominated the landscape. At the same time sand dunes, wide beaches, and extensive tidal flats remind us of the sculpting and levelling might of the ocean, which despite human efforts to tame it, continues to do what it has always done — shape the adjoining land.

The Atlantic region is separated from the rest of Canada by the Appalachian mountain chain. The famous Percé Rock off the tip of the Gaspé Peninsula is a familiar example of a much-eroded remnant of a once-great mountain, a long-pummelled and beaten vertebra of Appalachia. These mountains were once as magnificent as the Rockies; today they merely add character to the comparatively gentle topography of eastern North America.

LIFE ZONES

The Atlantic shore, with its red cliffs and wide, white beaches, its tide pools and starfish, its mobs of sandpipers and its frozen winters and lashing storms, is more than a topographic, climatic, and aesthetic phenomenon. It is a *community* consisting of more than land forms, more than crabs, codfish and puffins, more than plankton and kelp, more than the rush of a tidal soup. A community is an entity that is always more than the sum of its parts.

The notion of community is central to natural history and to ecology. This is not a new idea; naturalists have always known that there were apparent associations between the lay of the land, the climate, and the plants and animals. They have always known that in certain kinds of places you could expect to find certain kinds of living things, and that you were wasting your time looking elsewhere for those same things. Clearly a desert has different flora and fauna than a seacoast or a woodlot. But for centuries no one thought about it much more than that.

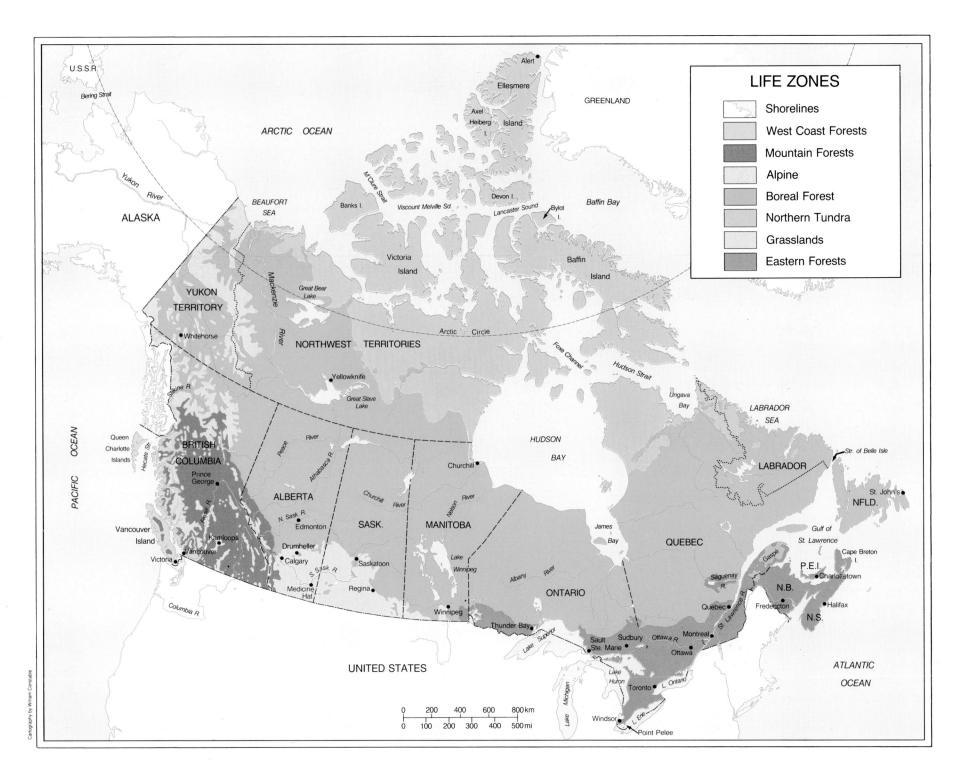

LIFE ZONES

- Shorelines
- West Coast Forests
- Mountain Forests
- Alpine
- Boreal Forest
- Northern Tundra
- Grasslands
- Eastern Forests

U.S.S.R.

Bering Strait

ARCTIC OCEAN

GREENLAND

ALASKA

BEAUFORT SEA

Yukon River

Alert

Ellesmere

Axel Heiberg I. *Island*

Banks I. *Viscount Melville Sd.* *Devon I.*

Lancaster Sound *Bylot I.*

Baffin Bay

YUKON TERRITORY

Mackenzie River

Great Bear Lake

Victoria Island

Baffin Island

• Whitehorse

NORTHWEST TERRITORIES

Arctic Circle

Foxe Channel

Hudson Strait

Stikine R.

• Yellowknife

Great Slave Lake

Ungava Bay

LABRADOR SEA

PACIFIC OCEAN

Queen Charlotte Islands

Hecate Str.

BRITISH COLUMBIA

Peace River

Athabasca R.

HUDSON BAY

• Churchill

LABRADOR

Str. of Belle Isle

Prince George •

ALBERTA

Churchill River

Nelson River

St. John's •

NFLD.

Vancouver Island

Fraser R.

Kamloops •

• Edmonton

N. Sask. R.

SASK.

MANITOBA

James Bay

QUEBEC

Gulf of St. Lawrence

Gaspé

Cape Breton I.

Vancouver •

Victoria •

Drumheller •

• Calgary

• Saskatoon

• Regina

Lake Winnipeg

Albany River

Saguenay R.

P.E.I.

• Charlottetown

N.B.

Medicine Hat •

S. Sask. R.

ONTARIO

Quebec •

Fredericton •

Halifax •

Columbia R.

Winnipeg •

Montreal •

St. Lawrence R.

N.S.

Thunder Bay •

Sault Ste. Marie •

Sudbury •

Ottawa R.

Ottawa •

UNITED STATES

Lake Superior

Toronto •

L. Ontario

ATLANTIC OCEAN

Lake Michigan

Lake Huron

L. Erie

Windsor •

Point Pelee

0   200   400   600   800 km
0   100   200   300   400   500 mi

Cartography by William Constable

Almost exactly 100 years ago, the American ornithologist C. Hart Merriam happened to be doing biological surveys in Arizona for the United States federal government. Arizona's rich fauna and dramatic topography make it attractive to naturalists. Especially interesting is the fact that you can climb up a steep mountainside and encounter many quite different plants and animals on the way up even though you only travel a short distance. Merriam pondered this; a realization dawned. The mountainside was *stratified* ; it was a series of rather distinct layers of plants and animals. Even more, the vertical progression of these zones was similar to the progression of continental zones from the Arizona desert northward to the pole. In both cases, the differences in these "life zones" were a function of temperature.

The detailed temperature-based zones proposed by Merriam did not completely stand up continentally, mainly because of broad climate patterns such as those of the prairies. But that is not important. His identification of life zones on the mountain slope was correct. At the time, he did not know that rocky seacoast shores and tropical rain forests, among other communities, were also vertically zoned.

Since Merriam's studies a number of terms have arisen to describe natural communities of various sizes and compositions, but here we shall stick with the original term *life zone* to describe a particular natural community visible and identifiable on the basis of the inter-related, interdependent plants and animals which together constitute it. In the remainder of the book we shall visit eight major life zones, most of which are further subdivided by special characteristics.

43

LIFE ZONES

Seabird Rookeries: The seabird sanctuary at Cape St. Mary's on the southwestern tip of Newfoundland's Avalon Peninsula is breeding ground for thousands of gannets, kittiwakes, and murres. During spring and early summer, seabirds fill the sky near the cliffs, hovering, diving, and flashing by at eye level; and the air is heavy with the metallic roar of countless birds squawking, growling, and screaming.

The Shorelines

Atlantic Puffin: Beak stuffed with capelin, an Atlantic puffin prepares to feed its young hidden in a nearby burrow. The puffin's existence along the Atlantic coast is threatened by depletion of capelin stocks from overfishing and the oil-spill risk posed by offshore oil development.

Samuel de Champlain was the first to record it: "The abundance of birds of different kinds is so great that no one would believe it possible unless he had seen it." It was May 1604; bird migration was at its peak, and he was in a major flyway. As well, there were thousands of breeding birds on a group of small islands off the southern tip of Nova Scotia. Champlain listed, "cormorants, ducks of three kinds, snow-geese, murres, wild geese, puffins, snipe, fish-hawks and other birds of prey, seagulls, plover of two or three kinds, herons, herring gulls, curlews, turnstones, divers, loons, eiders, ravens...." Of one island he reported: "We saw so great a number of birds called *tangeaux* [gannets] that we killed them easily with a stick. On another we found the shore completely covered with seals, whereof we took as many as we wished."

There are no gannets on those islands today, and there may not be the same numbers of cormorants on Green Island, near Cape Sable, which Champlain calls "the Isle of Cormorants... so named because of the infinite number of these birds, of whose eggs we took a barrel full." However, there are still plenty of cormorants around the Atlantic coast. There are also spectacular gannetries in the Gulf of St. Lawrence and along the outer coast of Newfoundland. But the numbers of both have shrunk terribly in the wake of Champlain's questing spirit.

With the exception of the gannets on Bonaventure Island off the tip of the Gaspé Peninsula, the major Atlantic seabird colonies nowadays are quite remote. When we manage to get to them, we marvel just as

Northern Gannet: Even with a wingspan of almost two metres, a northern gannet's landing is seldom soft. Flapping furiously, it drops clumsily into the crowded nesting colony, creating a brief, but vicious squabble should it overshoot its territory. Take-offs are not much smoother even though colonies are located on high cliffs to help launch the birds. Airborne, however, the gannet's behaviour is nothing less than spectacular. Sailing 25 metres above the sea on a fishing foray, it suddenly folds its wings and dives steeply into the water at speeds of 100 kilometres per hour. A thick skull and air cells in the bird's neck and breast, which are inflated prior to take-off, cushion the impact. The gannet may plunge into the water 20 metres, catching its prey on the upsweep and swallowing it just before surfacing.

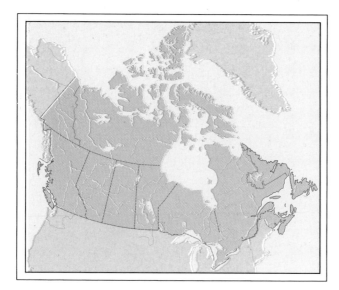

THE SHORELINES

the early explorers did. There are so many birds that it is difficult to grasp the extent of the food supply required to sustain them. For example, at the peak of the nesting cycle on Bonaventure, there may be 100,000 voracious, goose-sized northern gannets, each with an apparently insatiable appetite for herring, capelin, squid, and mackerel.

Of course a lot of animals have a taste for herring, capelin, squid, and mackerel. Several other species of seabirds, as well as codfish, salmon, seals, basking sharks, and baleen whales avail themselves of stupendous quantities of these. The total consumption is incalculable. It is more useful to think of these small food species not in numbers but in volume. In their annual appearances they surge into coastal waters like torrential flows of lava, rushing in their hordes to nourish populations of larger animals. There are millions of gullets of all sizes to be satisfied.

Consider the blue whale, the largest animal that has ever lived. For these whales, members of the baleen group, strainers take the place of teeth. The strainers are long, fibrous plates suspended from the

48

upper jaw and palate. They are of a keratinous material like that of hair, horns, claws, and hoofs. The whale opens its mouth, takes in seawater and whatever may be in it, strains it, and retains the food. The blue whale and its cousins, the fin, sei, minke, and humpback, have huge distensible throats, thanks to long, accordion-like pleats which extend from the tip of the lower jaw almost to the navel. When feeding, the whale relaxes these pleats, allowing a stupendous inflow of water. The throat then compresses, the gigantic tongue forces the water out through the baleen, and the catch is swallowed.

If the quantities of small animals consumed is difficult to grasp, then the abundance of plankton in cold Atlantic waters is beyond the imagination altogether. For it is plankton that supports everything else. We should consider plankton not as a flow or torrent, as with the fishes and squids, but as a vast three-dimensional pasture composed of myriads of microscopic plants and animals which are grazed upon by other animals. Microscopic they may be, but in their billions upon billions they become visible as a mass of larvae, minute crustaceans, and miniscule fishes. Ultimately, every living thing in and of the sea depends on plankton.

At the edge of the sea lies one of the richest and most varied habitats imaginable — the intertidal zone. Doused repeatedly by plankton-rich waters, this habitat (lying between high and low tide lines) makes special demands on the organisms that live there. Those demands derive partly from the physical nature of the coastline, be it a rocky shore, mudflat, sandy beach, boulder-strewn cove, gravel bed, or salt marsh. However, the nature of the shoreline is of secondary importance to the twice-a-day regime of drying and flooding. To live between the tides is to live precariously, unless one has special ways of coping. For those that manage to persist under such conditions, there is the reward of a constant flow of nourishment delivered with each wave.

Intertidal existence presents plants and animals with a difficult choice: either tolerate being dried out on a twice-daily basis, or somehow keep in touch with the diminished water level at low tide. They must also withstand violent, powerful, and continuous beating from waves. Furthermore, intertidal species must deal with constant shifting in the very base they rest on. Erosion never stops.

The trick for many animals — barnacles, mussels, and limpets for example — is to stay put under the fearsome pounding of the surf, and at the same time protect themselves from drying out. If they are mobile enough, they can move up and down with the water. Anemones, crabs, and starfish do just that. Not many plants can survive in the intertidal zone, and those that do have managed to grasp a firm roothold beneath the loose material on the bottom.

Pools of seawater often are left behind by the ebbing tide, and these provide sanctuary for some particularly fragile animals. But even these are not home free; they must be prepared for an increase in both light and warmth that comes with life in these still, shallow enclaves. The shoreline when exposed at low tide shows a conspicuous zonation, from top to bottom, of animals that are most to least tolerant of extremes of light, temperature, and dryness. At the top of the zone and firmly cemented to the rock are the barnacles. Enduring the longest exposure to the air, their lids are clamped shut, retaining sufficient seawater within to keep them going until high tide.

Humpback Whale: When a humpback makes its slow and graceful tail salute, it usually means it is heading down for an extended dive. Submerged, the whale feeds on inch-long krill (shrimp-like crustaceans) or small fish such as capelins, anchovies, and sardines. It plunges through these schools mouth agape, taking in whatever lies in its path. One humpback was found with four cormorants in its stomach, probably swallowed by mistake as the birds fished in the same area.

51

Just below the barnacles is the rockweed zone. Here among the drooping vegetation are legions of periwinkles and clusters of blue mussels. At all levels there are countless numbers of tiny crustaceans and other small invertebrates moving rhythmically back and forth, up and down, with the undulations of the sea. On rocky shores crabs seek out holes and crevices; on sand, many of them burrow.

During migration skeins of shorebirds — plovers, sandpipers, and their kindred — set down along both rocky and sandy shores to feed delicately on the small-est of these creatures of the water's edge. Systematically probing, poking, picking, and prying, they find a feast that is invisible to the human eye, but clearly of monumental abundance, bearing in mind the sheer numbers of feeders. There are great blue herons in all seasons, snatching fish from the tide pools and shallows. Beyond the surf, screaming terns dart and dash and flurry at the surface in pursuit of small fishes. Slightly bigger fishes are chased by puffins and other auks which, like penguins, virtually "fly" underwater. A fish of somewhat larger size is a

Grand Manan: The largest island in the Bay of Fundy, Grand Manan is located 27 kilometres off the New Brunswick mainland. At the base of the cliffs the rocky intertidal zone, draped with seaweeds, is exposed. Some of the seaweeds have bulbs that help them float free of the rocks when the returning tide begins to toss them about. Seaweeds secrete a lubricating slime that allows them to rub over rocks and one another without damage and limits dehydration when they are exposed to air.

Dogwhelks and Barnacles: Common animals of the intertidal zone, dogwhelks and barnacles have special mechanisms and behaviours to cope with the amphibious demands of their habitat. Barnacles have hard, calcerous plates (shown closed in photo) which they shut when the tide is out to prevent loss of critical body moisture. At high tide these hatches open and the barnacle's feathery legs reach out to feed on the plankton the tide brings in. Unlike the barnacle, which is permanently cemented to the rock, the dogwhelk, a snail-like mollusc, can move about when left high and dry to find water pockets or take shelter in the moist jungle of seaweed.

Harbour Seal: These curious marine mammals are found along most of Canada's shoreline with the exception of the western arctic. There are also landlocked populations of harbour seals on lakes in British Columbia and northern Quebec. In evolving to an aquatic existence the harbour seal has become streamlined, taking on the cigar shape of a tuna and losing its external ears and most of the size and strength of its forelimbs. These adaptations help it to hurtle through the water after fish to depths up to 300 metres for 20 minutes at a time.

Moresby Island: This rock shoreline on South Moresby Island of the Queen Charlottes is ideal habitat for intertidal life. The cracks and fissures provide protection for many animals. Each has a different method of clinging to the rock to avoid being swept away by the surf. Blue mussels use a fibrous network of tough hairs, barnacles are anchored with a glue as strong as the rock itself, limpets and sea stars are attached with airtight suction, and crabs crouch into a low, streamlined profile and latch on with grappling hook legs.

target for a cormorant cruising gracefully beneath the surface, or for the breath-taking plunge of a gannet, or for the snap of a seal.

No one who has ever looked a harbour seal in the eye could deny that animals have personality. There is an alertness, an intelligence, and just a dash of mischief. In spite of their familiarity with human activity in coastal waters, these seals are notably shy and self-effacing. Found along the Atlantic, Pacific, and Arctic coasts, they are the most widely distributed seals in Canada. Small numbers of them are landlocked in British Columbia and in the Ungava Peninsula in northern Quebec, but most inhabit sheltered bays, and rocky shores and beaches. Harbour seals are not migratory; unlike many of their relatives they stay in the same coastal waters year round.

WEST COAST

The tufted puffin looks even more clownish than its Atlantic counterpart, its raffish locks adding an extra dimension of jocularity. But as everyone knows, clowns take their business very seriously, and the demeanour of all puffins is earnestness itself. This odd looking seabird nests from Japan northward along the coast of Siberia, across the top of the Bering Sea, then south on the Alaska and British Columbia coasts to California.

Canada's Pacific waters are considerably warmer than those of the Atlantic coast which are chilled by the arctic flow of the Labrador Current. The warm waters of the Japanese Current and the prevailing westerly winds across the Pacific bathe the entire British Columbia coastline in mild temperatures. Nonetheless, the Pacific shoreline shares many of the biological processes and characteristics of the Atlantic.

Tides along the Pacific coast, especially around Vancouver Island, are not as regular as on the Atlantic coast. Of the two daily tides, one is more extreme than

Tufted Puffin: A tufted puffin approaches its burrow on Flat Rock Island in the southern Queen Charlotte Islands. The puffin's bill is brightly coloured during the spring and summer breeding season, but by winter the outer layers have been shed and the bill is smaller and more drab. Canada's largest tufted puffin colony is on Triangle Island off the north end of Vancouver Island.

the other. The effect is a broader range of intertidal habitat than in the Atlantic, and thanks to the prevalence of rocky shores, a richer and more diverse variety of plants and animals. For example, one can find about 130 more species of algae along the Pacific than the Atlantic coast. Indeed, the Pacific coast of North America has the greatest number of species of any temperate shore.

The Pacific intertidal area is zoned the same way as the Atlantic, with the highest levels occupied by those life forms that can tolerate dryness and sunlight, the bottom ones by those that must keep moist. Just above the high tide mark there is usually a blackish band along the rocks. This consists of lichens that can survive in the open air provided they receive some wetness from splattering and splashing. Around the high tide mark there are periwinkles. These small snails survive between high tides in much the same way as barnacles: by clamping shut and retaining a supply of moisture within their shells. Also at the high tide mark, or just above in the splash zone, are the limpets. These drab, flattened, snail-like creatures can withstand the heaviest pounding by the surf. And although they appear to be permanently fastened to their perches, they do move, albeit slowly and furtively. At the midway point of the intertidal zone are clusters of mussels clinging to the rocks by a network

57

Purple Sea Stars: Blind, toothless, and slow-moving, the sea star is an unlikely predator. Yet it prowls the intertidal zone relentlessly in search of clams and mussels. Its long arms, lined with hundreds of tiny suction cups, encircle its prey and gradually pry open its protective shell. With grotesque efficiency, the sea star then extrudes its sac-like stomach through its mouth and into the vulnerable flesh of the victim, digesting it on the spot.

Great Blue Heron: Tidal pools and shallows are favoured fishing grounds for great blue herons along the Pacific coast. They remain motionless, poised atop long, reed-like legs until a fish swims near. Then they strike with lightning speed.

of fibrous hairs. They are a favourite food of surf scoters and also black oystercatchers which chisel them free with long, gaudy orange bills. At the same level are the chitons, tiny ovals of calcareous plates and tough flesh which cling in much the same manner as limpets.

Throughout the intertidal area of both coasts are the seaweeds, some of which may be rooted close to the high tide mark, thus needing to survive long periods out of the water. They may become quite hard and brittle when dry, but take up water and swell back to normal once the tide rises. Some sea plants can tolerate no drying out and survive only in permanent tide pools or below the lowest tide. One of the more noteworthy of these is the coralline seaweed, a pinkish plant that looks more like an encrusted coral or a lichen. This plant is an important source of nourishment for sea urchins, which need lime to maintain their skeletal structures. Also below low tide, their root-bases never exposed to the air, are the sea lettuces, the kelps, and the lavers, red algae which are often gathered for human food.

The brightest treasures found in tide pools, or beneath rock where sufficient moisture remains, are the sea stars and brittle stars in vivid colours — violet, purple, yellow, brown, or pink. Some sea stars range as high as the mussel beds and can endure temporary

Orca Whale: The inner coast of Vancouver Island has one of the world's most concentrated populations of orcas, or killer whales. This bull, recognized by his two metre dorsal fin, is member of a pod that resides in Johnstone Strait year round. Such resident whales feed mainly on fish and occasionally congregate in certain coves to rub their bellies on pebble beaches.

exposure, although most prefer to remain submerged. Brittle stars, with their thin, elongated arms, can tolerate neither air nor light. They abound in sheltered places and on the sea floor where they consume scraps of dead animals and other debris.

Sea stars and brittle stars are echinoderms, the spiny-skinned ones for whom five is the magic number. Many have five arms. Their relative, the sea urchin, with its waving spines, is also built on a five-sided format as is the sea cucumber, which belongs to the same group. Urchins are formidable little creatures, and some can give your naked foot a nasty wound. They are one of the dietary mainstays, at least in some places, of the gentle, comical sea otter.

Wrapped in kelp fronds offshore, sea otters loll about on their backs much of the time. The living is easy, and there is plenty of time for loafing. Although sea urchins may represent three-quarters of their diet, they also consume mussels in considerable quantity, the shells of which the sea otter will crack open with a rock, using its chest as an anvil, while floating on its back. Hunted almost to extinction early in this century in British Columbia (it is not found on the Atlantic coast), this much-loved species has been reintroduced along the northwest coast of Vancouver Island and now appears to be breeding successfully.

Although otters are members of the weasel family, sea otters have lived a marine existence for so long that they look and act surprisingly like small fur seals. They loll about on their backs and play at the surface in much the same way. Northern fur seals do not breed in Canada (their famous rookeries are in the Pribilof Islands of Alaska), but they are often seen along the British Columbia coast during the winter and in spring and fall migrations. Their cousin, the northern sea lion, is a year round resident.

Fur seals and sea lions, also Pacific specialities, are "eared" seals and have a number of differences from "true" seals. They still get about reasonably well on land, thanks to rear limbs which can be rotated forward for locomotion. In the water eared seals propel themselves with strokes from their powerful front flippers, whereas true seals swim with a wiggling, fish-like action. Northern sea lions occur from Japan to the Bering Sea and all the way south to California. From time to time they receive a good deal of notoriety in British Columbia because of their alleged depredations on salmon. The fact is that these immense animals (big males may weigh a tonne) are nearly non-stop feeders, and they take pretty much whatever they can get. A.W.F. Banfield, in *The Mammals of Canada*, lists sea lion food items that are worth quoting for their sheer variety: "Coelenterates, sand dollars, worms, molluscs, crabs, squid and octopus, lamprey, pollack, flounders, sculpins, cod, herring, skate and dogfish, sea perch, halibut, salmon, sable fish, eulachon, rockfish, hake, greenling, and lumpfish." Banfield also relates the story of two sea lions, killed at the height of a salmon run, whose stomach contents were exclusively and surprisingly lamprey. There is no doubt, though, that they do damage fishing gear and at least sometimes avail themselves of fish already caught in commercial nets. Punitive action against sea lions, or agitation for it, appears to be part of the west coast tradition.

Apart from ourselves, the only significant enemy of the sea lion along the Pacific coast is the "killer" whale. This unfortunate and misleading colloquial name for what is probably the most magnificent animal in the sea should be forgotten and replaced with

the proper name, orca. These remarkable beasts are often seen travelling in family groups, or pods, close to shore. This is the only whale in the world whose diet is primarily warm-blooded animals, including grey whales, minke whales, walruses, beluga whales, and seals. No doubt that is why it was labelled "killer"; cold-blooded animals such as fishes and squids don't seem to qualify for human concern. One observer tells of a pod which began vigorously harassing a sea lion, repeatedly charging at it, knocking it high out of the water with their flukes, and generally terrorizing the hapless creature. Even more remarkable, the commotion was joined by a pair of humpback whales which soon became as excited as the orcas, and moved among them freely. Finally a cow and calf humpback joined the orcas, the parent apparently showing no concern for her little one. By the end of this episode, there were five humpback whales within 100 metres of the orcas, and the sea lion was nowhere in sight. The encounter between the humpbacks and the orcas in this instance had been entirely non-violent.

Orcas eat some of the larger fishes, and along the British Columbia coast that means salmon. When the homeward migrations of salmon are at their peak, the orcas fare very well; no doubt they also do some net-rending. Most of the salmon eating is done by whales that live along the coast year round; transient orcas seem to concentrate more on sea mammals.

As salmon approach the estuaries of their natal streams and enter shallow water, large predators onshore await them. Of these the most impressive is the grizzly bear, recognized by its humped shoulders, dished-in face, and enormous claws. It is much bigger than a black bear and more powerfully built. Solitary much of the time, these great creatures can be seen in numbers only where there is a special food attraction. Such an event is the salmon run, when spawning and spawned-out fish can be easily caught. Where there is an abundance of fish, bears gorge themselves only on the finest delicacies, especially the eggs. There are plenty of gulls, wolves, black bears, raccoons, and bald eagles to consume the rest.

The Pacific coast has the largest population of bald eagles remaining in Canada. This superb species was once common along the Atlantic coast as well, but relatively few remain today. Along the British Columbia shoreline, there is everything for its needs — large trees for nesting, a seemingly inexhaustible food source of fish and seabirds, and perhaps most important of all, appreciation and watchfulness by the general public.

Grizzly and Gulls: In late summer and fall grizzlies gorge themselves on salmon that move up coastal rivers to spawn. They sometimes eat the whole carcass, or if fish are plentiful they feast on the brains and eggs. The Khutzeymateen River north of Prince Rupert is prime habitat for grizzlies which feed on both the salmon and lush vegetation of the delta and river banks.

The West Coast Forests

Goldstream River: Big-leaf maple leaves are scattered over the shallows of the Goldstream River on southern Vancouver Island. This small river, its banks lined by coastal rain forest, supports a sizeable chum salmon run.

The wondrous story of the Pacific salmon reaches its climax beneath the moss-draped boughs of British Columbia's coastal rain forest. The life cycle of the five salmon species has been well documented — their hatching in interior streams and lake beds, their early days as alevins (consisting mostly of eyes and a food sac) hidden in the gravel, their emergence as fry, their period of growth in fresh water, their journey downstream and years in the open sea, and then their eventual return to their fresh water birthplaces as adults, their spawning, and their death.

The final stages of this timeless saga are the most dramatic. After heading toward land from the vastness of the ocean, the adult fish somehow pick out the taste of their natal streams from among thousands of conflicting and confusing signals in the inshore waters. Consider that one large river, diluting the salt with its enormous volumes of rain and meltwater from the interior, will have many major tributaries and hundreds of minor feeders, one of which is the salmon's natal stream. And there are numerous very substantial rivers, dozens of smaller ones. Nonetheless, the salmon pick up the beacon for which they have been scanning, and rush toward the gaping mouth of the river of their origin and destiny.

As the salmon approach the coast, they enter what must seem a most incongruous environment for free-ranging ocean fish. The rocky river mouth, its precipitous sides ripped and shorn by the glaciers, its walls mantled in deep green, is a formidable entrance to the mountain citadel. Here the

Chum Salmon: Every fall British Columbia's coastal streams are littered with dying salmon which have spawned and completed their life cycle.

65

Cougar: The drooping branches of a western red cedar obscure the tawny form of a cougar. This secretive, nocturnal cat is relatively numerous in the west coast forests, especially on Vancouver Island where 80 percent of its diet is comprised of Columbian blacktail deer. Springing onto the deer's back, the cougar bites deeply into the victim's neck killing it quickly.

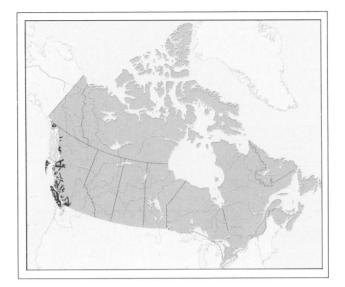

THE WEST COAST FORESTS

forest along the shoreline is dominated by towering Sitka spruce.

Although the Sitka spruce is not the largest of the rain forest trees, it is by far the largest of the spruces. Many reach two metres in diameter and 50 metres in height. Occasional giants have measured almost four metres in diameter and 75 metres in height. Where a stand of these trees is dense, their trunks soar upward cleanly and without branching — a timberman's dream. These huge trees grow only near the coast, rarely more than 80 kilometres inland, and seldom at elevations of more than 300 metres. This is the only rain forest tree whose range is so restricted to the shoreline.

Rain forest is a term usually reserved for the broadleaved tropics. But in British Columbia, specifically on the Queen Charlotte Islands, along the west coast of Vancouver Island, and on the mainland coast, a luxuriant rain forest thrives. This immense forest is the result of a long growing

Sitka Spruce: On Moresby Island in the Queen Charlottes, a grove of mossy Sitka spruce characterizes the lush coastal rain forest. Never found far from the sea, the Sitka spruce's long straight trunk and tough wood make it a prized tree of loggers.

season, a gentle maritime climate, and lots of rain — up to four metres a year. The soils are generally deep and well drained; mosses and ferns are abundant. And the trees are legendary. They are the largest and oldest in Canada — many have been here for more than 500 years, some more than 1,000. The characteristic species are western red cedar, western hemlock, Douglas-fir, and Sitka spruce.

Some botanical clarification is required here. There are no true cedars in Canada, or in North America. The western red cedar and the eastern white cedar are arbor-vitae. What is called "red cedar" in the east is actually a juniper. What is known as "yellow cedar" in the west is actually a cypress. Here we will use the colloquial terms.

What name we choose to attach to a living being, however, is of no importance. So long as the western red cedars are left to their own devices which include rich, moist soils, a cool climate, and perhaps 800 years to reach maturity, it matters not what we call them. After all, human lexicons, languages, and cultural perceptions will change profoundly over the lifetime of a single tree. Many of the trees we fell today were alive before there was Middle English.

At the northern tip of Vancouver Island, once a wild land of deer, wolf, and cougar, the ineffable magnificence of the coast forest can still be enjoyed in some of the unlogged areas. Here are the largest trees in Canada, and the greatest of them all is the Douglas-fir. Soaring even higher than the red cedars and hemlocks, this most supreme of our tree species has been known to tower some 90 metres and reach 4.5 metres in diameter. Individuals have lived to the age of 1,200 years.

Salmonberry: A common shrub of the rain forest, salmonberry has flowers that appear as early as February. The blooming period is so long that flowers and fruit can sometimes be found on the same bush. The edible but tart berries ripen to either a ruby red or salmon colour.

Rufous Hummingbird: Although not as brilliantly coloured as her male counterpart, the female rufous hummingbird is the same master of flight, able to hover and fly backward, sideways, and forward at amazing speeds. She builds her nest in a low branch of a conifer. The tiny cup, barely five centimetres wide, is bound with spider's silk, lined with plant down, moss, and strips of bark, and camouflaged on the outside with lichens. Here she lays two, bean-sized eggs.

69

Most of British Columbia's magnificent forests of old-growth Douglas-fir were cut during the last century. Today there are a few remnant stands, most notably at Cathedral Grove and in the Nimp-kish Valley on Vancouver Island. Impressive as these Douglas-firs may appear, they are only temporary species in the rain forest. Douglas-fir seedlings cannot grow in the shade of their parent trees and are eventually replaced by shade-tolerant western hemlocks and red cedar — species that, barring fires, will eventually dominate the forest community.

One encounters the amabilis fir on well-drained sites throughout the rain forest, except for the Queen Charlotte Islands. This is not a giant tree, but a respectable one nonetheless, averaging about a metre in diameter and reaching more than 30 metres in height. Above elevations of 350 to 400 metres, red cedar and Sitka spruce disappear, and mountain hemlock begins to replace western hemlock. At higher elevations yellow cedar begins to take over. Its range extends well beyond the coast forest to the point where it is found as little more than a crawling shrub among the rocks in the most inhospitable and bleak exposures. Lodgepole pine (shore pine) is similarly adaptable to extreme situations. It grows from treeline right down to sea level in bogs and other difficult sites unsuitable for most other conifers.

The only deciduous tree of any size in the coast forests is the big-leaf maple, so named for a leaf that may be 30 centimetres wide. It is entirely shade-tolerant, growing in the moist, rich, cool understorey of the great conifers. Some of these maples reach a very respectable height — up to 30 metres — but since its benefactors are likely twice that height, the maple does not receive the recognition it would if it were growing in an eastern

Yellow Cedars: Draped with mosses and lichens, yellow cedars are usually found at higher elevations in the west coast forests. These slow-growing conifers may require 200 years to reach full stature. Some gnarled specimens are 1.5 metres in diameter and more than 1,000 years old — perhaps the oldest trees in Canada.

71

woodlot. Straight-trunked stands do attract the attention of loggers, however. The other two maple species of British Columbia, the Douglas and vine maple, are little more than shrubs that rarely reach tree size.

Mosses and ferns abound in these wet forests; beside streams and in bottomlands there is red alder, and in sunny locations, black cottonwood. The best-known shrubs of the area are salal, salmonberry, and devil's club. Salal is profuse throughout the coastal forests, and depending on the site, it may be thinly scattered, low cover or a fiendishly difficult tangle three metres high. The thick, pointed leaves are evergreen and exceedingly tough, the stems unusually strong, resulting in a worthy challenge for the most determined hiker. Backpackers who stray from established trails are

Vine Maple: Favouring moist soils along the banks of streams, vine maple grows in the coast forest. Although often remaining a coarse shrub, under good conditions vine maple will grow into a medium-sized tree. Its leaves are distinctive in having the largest number of lobes of any native maple in Canada. In autumn, vine maple leaves add a splash of colour to the evergreen coastal forest.

likely, as well, to find their route barricaded by salmonberry shrubs armed with stiff prickles. The fragile, magenta blooms of salmonberry appear in mid-winter. Not quite as abundant is devil's club, which grows along the coast wherever it is sufficiently moist for red cedars. Its large leaves look something like those of a maple, and its unusually thick stems are festooned with sharp spines. It produces bright red berries in late summer.

Cut off by the formidable barrier of the Coast Mountains, many animals of the coast forest have evolved in isolation from their inland relatives and are represented by distinctive subspecies. Columbian blacktail deer are smaller versions of the mule deer found inland. Well adapted to coastal life, they do not hesitate to swim across saltwater straits to reach better forage.

Deer of the coast forest (and wapiti on Vancouver Island) are fed upon by wolves. Wolves live mostly in family groups. The "lone wolf" may occur occasionally, but a single animal does not survive long. Wolves are not as swift of foot as their prey and must hunt strategically and cooperatively in packs. They have developed a system of hunting and other social behaviour the sophistication of which is just beginning to be discovered.

Through the centuries the wolf has been feared and greatly misunderstood. Campaigns for its extermination in Canada have been defended on grounds that it competes with humans for the meat of hoofed animals. Wolves, however, require that meat for survival; humans want it for recreational killing. The dependence of predator numbers on the numbers of prey, and the normal inability of predators to affect prey populations, is consciously ignored. The war against the wolf continues in the interest of the relationship between tourist outfitters and politicians.

Columbian Blacktail Deer: In the west coast forests, the mule deer is represented by a small subspecies, the Columbian blacktail deer. Their diet varies with habitat but they generally browse on Douglas-fir, western red cedar, salal, and trailing blackberry supplemented in summer by a range of herbs. Older bucks begin to grow new antlers in April, and by September they are fully developed. As the bucks rub their antlers against brush and joust with saplings, their neck muscles become enlarged, not only from exercise but from an increase in tissue fluid.

Blue Grouse: Inhabiting coniferous forests at higher elevations during the winter, blue grouse descend into the valleys in spring to nest in clearings and logging slash. The cock issues a powerful, ventriloquistic hooting, almost impossible to pinpoint, to announce his readiness to mate. His message, broadcast from high in a tree, can be heard for kilometres around.

The rain forest on the Queen Charlotte Islands is biologically unique. Not only do the islands contain magnificent stands of giant conifers (preserved in South Moresby National Park), they also possess some faunal peculiarities. The blue grouse in the Queen Charlottes, although closely related to the coastal mainland form, is characterized by a much redder hue. The only owl on the islands, a dark reddish form of the northern saw-whet, has been classified as racially distinct from saw-whets in the rest of Canada. Another specialty is the black bear. This is a larger and more massive race than those of the mainland. Other rarities include many kinds of stickleback fish, several flowering plants, and varieties of mosses and liverworts. These life forms survived on the Queen Charlottes while their relatives on the mainland succumbed to the last glaciation.

The animal you would least expect to find on the Queen Charlotte Islands is the western toad. It

Devil's Club: This shrub with its spiked stems and large maple-shaped leaves is likely to be found in damp, soft soil where western red cedar grows. The small, greenish flowers appear in June and develop into clusters of bright red berries by August.

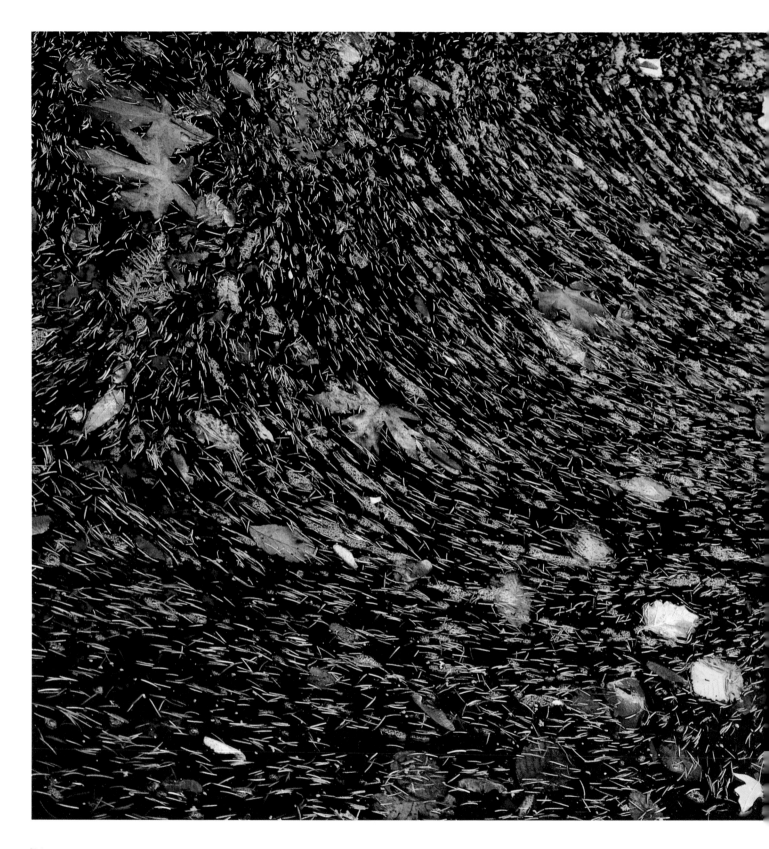

Stream Litter: The needles and leaves of Douglas-fir, western hemlock, big-leaf maple, and red alder — common trees of the west coast rain forest — swirl in a streamside pool on Vancouver Island. This fallen debris signals the approach of the mild, wet winter characteristic of the Pacific coast.

is not a rare animal but an offshore island is perhaps the last place an amphibian is likely to reach. Fifty kilometres, the shortest distance from the mainland, is far too much for any salt-sensitive frog or toad to swim and survive. Perhaps a raft of vegetative debris drifted to the Queen Charlottes with toads aboard. Or someone may have put the western toad there. In any case, this toad, along with the Pacific tree frog (known to have been introduced) appear to be the only amphibians on the Queen Charlottes.

The Pacific tree frog is no larger than a human thumb. But it has fame hugely disproportionate to its tiny size. It has probably performed on more Hollywood sound tracks than any other animal and is the source of the well-known "rib-it" sound. Apparently it was introduced to the Queen Charlottes because the child of a long-time resident liked to hear it sing. Male tree frogs begin singing in February when they congregate in open ponds, lakes, and swamps to breed. The sound, produced by a spherical, inflatable throat sac, attracts a sexually responsive female. Clusters of 500 or more eggs are laid and fertilized in the water and in one to five weeks the tadpoles emerge.

With the exception of the occasional giant leatherback or green sea turtle, which are summer wanderers from the south, there are no reptiles on the Queen Charlotte Islands.

GULF ISLANDS WOODLANDS

Along the southeast coast of Vancouver Island, on the Gulf Islands, and in the extreme southerly portion of the Fraser Valley, there is an area of much reduced rainfall which is so different from the rest of the Pacific coast region as to constitute a distinct biological community. It is generally called the Gulf Islands zone, although it is sometimes referred to as the Garry oak/arbutus, or the dry coastal region. By whatever name, it is a sunny, relatively dry pocket in an expanse of wet coastal forest.

This sunny area is the result of the rain shadow cast by the Vancouver Island mountain ranges and, to a greater extent, by the Olympic Mountains in Washington State. Moist Pacific weather systems dump most of their rain on the western seaward slopes. As a result, the Gulf Islands zone on the eastern "shadow" side remains relatively dry and sunny.

This zone is warm and dry enough even for cactus. Prickly-pear cactus, with its gorgeous yellow flowers, ekes out a living on some of the southernmost Gulf Islands. Here, as elsewhere in Canada where it is able to persist, the prickly-pear is dwarfed, rarely more than 10 centimetres tall.

The Garry oak, British Columbia's only native oak, is largely confined to this area. On wind-sheltered sites it can be a good-sized tree, up to a metre in diameter and perhaps 18 metres in height. But individuals of that size are rare today, most sheltered areas having been "developed" for human purposes. On wind-blown sites near the sea, this oak is much smaller, often little more than a gnarled and twisted shrub.

Like other oaks, the Garry likes its base well drained and will tolerate both gravelly and rocky conditions, as long as its roots are dry. It is rarely found in dense stands, preferring open spacing with plenty of room to assume its sprawling, shaggy form. And it does not mix with other trees; it may be near, but cannot be under Douglas-fir, for example. Its only regular associate is the arbutus, another tree species which in Canada is unique to this zone.

The arbutus is singular in a number of ways. It is Canada's only evergreen, broadleaved tree. The oval leaves are thick, leathery to the touch, and dark and glossy on the upper surface. Water runs off them readily, with the result that an icy coating cannot develop should the temperature dip below freezing. The arbutus's most noteworthy characteristic is its bark — coppery orange-red, brilliant in the sun, often peeling and shaggy, and unmistakable. Also distinctive is its form, with branches striking out in all directions and a trunk twisted and gnarled, frequently leaning precariously. The arbutus is not a large tree, even under the best conditions it is rarely more than 12 metres tall. It loves the sun and thrives on exposed rocky bluffs overlooking the sea. Occasionally you may come upon pure stands of this eye-catching species, but never above 300 metres in elevation.

No account of the flora of these dry woodlands would be complete without mention of the spectacular displays of wild flowering plants. Botanists on Vancouver Island list more than 25 species blooming in January alone. Indian plum with its drooping clusters of white flowers is among the

Sword Ferns: A large fern of the west coast forests, sword fern thrives on the shaded forest floor. Its evergreen leafy branches, called fronds, are resilient to cold and can withstand frost. They rise out of the ground rolled up like watch springs and slowly uncoil. Ferns are similar to flowering plants in having roots, stems, and leaf-like fronds. They reproduce, however, by means of air-borne, microscopic spores rather than seeds.

78

Garry Oak: Together with Douglas-fir and arbutus, Garry oak is one of the principal trees of the Gulf Islands woodlands. Although this zone receives only modest amounts of precipitation on a yearly basis, winters are quite wet. Swollen by rain and humid air, lichens proliferate covering branches with shaggy growths.

79

first to appear, followed by another shrub, red-flowered currant. Its blooming period begins in March and coincides with the arrival of rufous hummingbirds from their wintering grounds in Mexico.

With dazzling speed and flashes of fiery iridescence, the hummingbirds flit through the open woods in search of gnats, flies, spiders, and wildflowers. These super-charged jewels are so little and swift, that it takes a sharp eye to spot one. Your best bet is to watch the red-flowered currant shrubs where the hummingbirds congregate, hovering and even flying backwards as they manoeuvre among the blossoms. With a high metabolism and heart rate of over 500 beats per minute, the rufous hummingbird must eat almost continuously to avoid starvation.

The peak blooming period on the Gulf Islands and southern Vancouver Island occurs in April and May when the meadows and woodlands are a carnival of colour. Many of the blooms are as exotic as their names — shooting star, chocolate lily, and little monkey flower. Around the Garry oaks there are blue-purple clusters of camas and masses of Easter lilies standing white and gold above mottled leaves. On drier sites satin flowers glow reddish-purple for a period all the more precious for its brevity. And there are many more, all shimmering, shining, and glowing evidence of a magical mix of climate, topography, and life process.

White Fawn Lily: This graceful perennial thrives in a variety of habitats in the Gulf Islands zone, an area known for its profusion of spring wildflowers. These white fawn lilies and pink shooting stars enliven a woodland in Thetis Lake Park near Victoria.

Blue Camas: One of the most common wildflowers of this zone, camas washes meadows a startling blue-violet each spring. Although most abundant in the west, several species of camas are found in open meadows across Canada.

Sea Blush: A honey bee roams over a cluster of tiny pink flowers called sea blush. One of the first wildflowers to bloom in these woodlands, it grows on sunny rock knolls, often with blue-eyed Mary and stonecrop.

The Mountain Forests

Even on the coldest days, the song of the American dipper can be heard. Clear and melodious, the sound seems unusually loud, cutting as it does through the frigid silence. A mixture of rich trills and clear, flute-like notes, it is accompanied by the gentle tinkling of ice in moving water. Why the dipper sings year round nobody knows, though it is not the only bird to do so. In our determination to interpret bird song in terms of aggressive "territoriality", winter bird song is still considered an anomaly. What prompts a small, plain bird to give voice in the face of mountain winter? Could it be that dippers simply like to sing?

Although it ranges from Alaska south through the mountains and well into the United States, the American dipper seems especially to capture the feeling of the Columbia forest. The smallest region of the mountain forests zone, the Columbia forest occurs in British Columbia on the westward-facing mountain slopes east of the central plateaus. They receive large quantities of rain from Pacific air masses. The result is a forest cover which is similar to that of the Pacific coast, although individual trees are not quite so large, and there are not quite as many species.

The Columbia forest lies between 600 and about 1,400 metres in elevation. Geographically, this "transplanted" coastal wet forest occurs through much of the Kootenay River valley, the upper Fraser and Thompson River valleys, and the Quesnel Lake area. Another pocket grows farther to the northwest in the Nass and Skeena River drainages. The characteristic trees are the familiar ones from the west coast forests — western red cedar, western hemlock, and Douglas-fir.

Autumn Mountainside: Among the dark green spires of alpine fir, golden aspens catch the last light of day. Pale green blueberry shrubs, a few just beginning to show their fall colours, attract bears to these slopes. The mountain forest zone occupies most of the interior of British Columbia and the mountainous areas of western Alberta.

83

Columbia Mountains: The lower slopes of the Columbia Mountains and the western slopes of the Rockies comprise most of the Columbia forest zone. The high peaks of the Columbia Mountains intercept passing clouds causing much rain to fall in the valleys. Huge trees and lush forests, similar to those of the west coast, result.

THE MOUNTAIN FORESTS

Generally one finds Douglas-fir in the drier areas, cedar in the wetter spots, and hemlock on the choicest moist soils. Sitka spruce, bound to the sea, does not occur here.

The understorey is similar to that of the rain forest, except that salal is absent. There is plenty of devil's club to replace it. Other typical shrubs include false azalea, black and red twinberry, redberry elder, salmonberry, thimbleberry, and squashberry. Heart-leaf arnica, columbine, bunchberry, and mountain lily are some common flowers. In contrast to the west coast forest, the Columbia forest is cold, and in winter there is much snow.

At its highest elevation, where it meets the subalpine forest, there are mixed stands of white spruce and Douglas-fir. Farther south, the transition into montane forest can be seen. In these drier areas the common associate of Douglas-fir is the western larch, and lodgepole pine appears where there has been fire.

84

85

White Birch: Found throughout most of Canada including the mountain forest zone, white birch is variable in general form and leaf shape and has numerous subspecies. Its best known feature is the peeling, papery white bark which becomes thick and broken into rough segments as the tree ages. Although birch saplings cannot grow in shaded forests, they spring up quickly on areas opened up by logging, fire, or blowdowns.

Few mammals live exclusively in coniferous woods. The red squirrel is an exception, rarely venturing far from cone-bearing evergreens. Considering the amazing speed and agility of these small arboreal rodents, one cannot help but be impressed by the skills of those animals that catch them. Martens do, as well as sundry hawks and owls, foxes, coyotes, and weasels. Indeed almost every form of predator, reptiles and fishes included, has been known to devour red squirrels.

This seems reasonable in a way because the red squirrel itself feeds upon almost anything that comes along. Frequently it raids bird nests for eggs or nestlings, and also catches mice and a variety of invertebrates. But it is especially fond of all manner of conifer seeds — pine, larch, spruce, hemlock, Douglas-fir, or cedar. The red squirrel does not hibernate, so it must stash away cone supplies in burrows for the winter. There are reports that in the far north it may bed down for a few days during the most severe storms.

Larger predators, such as black bears, are also found in the Columbia forest. Although black bears range from coast to coast, the particular form that lives in this area is of special interest. It is a large race, in which two colour phases are almost equally common, the black and the brown (cinnamon). There seems to be no particular reason for the appearance of two colours beyond genetic happenstance.

In spite of its fearsome reputation and its value to some as trophy material "bravely" obtained, you can be quite confident that no bear is out to get you. Barring illness, the animal is dangerous only when frightened, and of course one of the things that can frighten it is when its offspring are endangered. Over three-quarters of its food is vegetable and fruit, the remainder is insects, carrion, and small mammals. The bear's liking for honey has always been conventional wisdom. But recent study suggests that what the beehive-marauding bear is really after are protein-rich bee larvae, and that tales of its sweet tooth, though undeniable to a degree, may have been exaggerated.

Bears range widely in the mountain forests. You can see them in the darkest depths of the wet forest, in coniferous, broadleaved, or mixed woods,

Red Squirrel: A treetop acrobat, the red squirrel races along narrow twisting branches, sometimes even upside down, and leaps spread-eagle to other trees falling many metres in the process. Such antics are not as dangerous as they seem; red squirrels have fallen more than 30 metres without injury. Bold, noisy, curious, and active all year long, a red squirrel needs a lot of food. In addition to all kinds of fruit and mushrooms, it eats insects, eggs, nestlings, mice, young cottontails, and even small birds. In spring it slashes the bark of maples to lick up sap or drives yellow-bellied sapsuckers away from their rows of borings. But the mainstay of the red squirrel's diet is conifer seeds. It gathers cones into huge piles that may be a metre deep and several metres across. By the end of summer, one squirrel may amass up to 14,000 cones. It protects its cache and its territory vigorously, stamping its feet, chattering, flicking its big tail, and chasing off intruders if possible.

87

Black Bear: With the possible exception of the coyote, the black bear is the most successful large carnivore in North America. Adaptability to a wide range of habitats and foods is the key to its success. The black bear has few natural enemies except for man who kills about 30,000 of them every year in North America. Its tree climbing ability, perhaps developed in a long-ago era when it was vulnerable to numerous giant predators now extinct, is the black bear's best defence against wolves and grizzlies, which may attack females and cubs.

Skunk Cabbage: The miniscule flowers of skunk cabbage are tightly clustered on a club-like structure called the spadix which itself is wrapped in a bright yellow hood called the spathe. Once the spathe begins to fade, the plant's waxy leaves shoot up, becoming by summer the largest of any native plant in the country, measuring up to a metre long and half a metre wide. Skunk cabbage is eaten by deer and black and grizzly bears.

Blueberries: In early summer blueberry shrubs are festooned with urn-shaped, pink flowers which develop into dark blue berries. The fruits are an important summer food for grouse, songbirds, chipmunks, and black and grizzly bears.

on open burns where berries are plentiful, in swamps and bottomlands, high on talus slopes, and sometimes on alpine and arctic tundra. Few mammals are so adept at accommodating themselves to a variety of habitats.

MONTANE FOREST

Montane forest is found generally on the dry, central plateau of British Columbia and in the sheltered mountain valleys of the southern Rockies. In its pure form, away from its borders with the Columbia and subalpine forests, montane forest is characterized by the interior Douglas-fir, a stockier, shorter version of the famous coastal form. In its southern portion the montane forest is often dominated by parklike stands of ponderosa pine. At the lowest elevations there are large patches of prairie grassland.

The ponderosa pine is best known for its strikingly patterned, reddish-brown bark whose heavy,

terracotta-like plates are separated by deep furrows. It can be a very big tree, some growing 50 metres high and almost two metres in diameter. But most reach little more than half these dimensions. The ponderosa tends to grow on very well-drained sites. Lacking an understorey of smaller tree species and all but the smallest shrubs, and with grass everywhere, these areas have an obvious parkland character.

Throughout the montane forest, as almost everywhere in British Columbia, the southern Yukon, and western Alberta, there are extensive areas of lodgepole pine. This slender tree usually grows in dense stands, the thin, straight trunks reaching 30 metres. Like its relative the jack pine east of the Rocky Mountains, the lodgepole is a fire-dependent species, its cones requiring intense heat before they open and release seeds.

When the transcontinental railbeds were being built through the mountains and in the years of settlement that followed, there were numerous forest fires. These burns greatly increased the proliferation of lodgepole pine so that it now covers extensive tracts throughout its range. Unfortunately, where there are major stands of this pine, there is very little else, with large mammals in particular tending to avoid them.

But there is lots to be seen in the more open areas of the montane forest, thanks to the abundance of grassy cover for voles and other small rodents which attract coyotes. Out "mousing" and unaware of your presence, a coyote is one of the loveliest sights in nature. In spite of its resemblance to a medium-sized dog, the coyote behaves more like breeze-wafted thistledown. It seems weightless, so light and delicate is its graceful bound into the air and stiff, four-legged pounce into the grass. The pointed nose, alert ears, and

Fraser River: Rushing through the interior plateau of central British Columbia, the Fraser River drains 238,000 square kilometres of rugged terrain. Montane forests of interior Douglas-fir and lodgepole pine grow along the dry river banks and valleys of this region.

91

Cinnamon Teal: A drake in nuptial plumage preens on a slough in one of the low valleys of the montane forest region of British Columbia.

Coyote: The shrill, squealing song of the coyote is usually an announcement of its territorial claims. Howling is almost always done in concert with other pack members, each individual adding volume to the serenade to increase the intimidating effect on rival packs. Although the coyote is found throughout the mountain forests and much of Canada, it is most common in the grasslands outside the range of its chief predator, the wolf. The coyote's predatory behaviour, which occasionally is directed at livestock, has made it the target of many extermination campaigns over the years. These attempts were largely unsuccessful and the coyote has survived in most of its original range and even expanded northward into the Yukon and Northwest Territories and eastward into southern Ontario, Quebec, New Brunswick, and Nova Scotia.

stiffened tail speak of quick intelligence and energy, extraordinary physical agility and coordination. Coyotes seem to have been created specifically to animate the open country with their airy, vole-hunting caprioles.

Although no large predator has the speed to catch a coyote on the flat, at times an unwary one falls victim to a black or grizzly bear, or a cougar, or perhaps several wolves chasing in tandem. Coyotes fear wolves for good reason; foxes fear coyotes for the same reason. Although the larger wild dogs will sometimes kill the smaller ones, they rarely eat the victim. No one seems to know why. On the other hand, on those rare occasions when a coyote is killed by a cougar, it will be consumed. Since cougars hunt by stealth, the coyote's speed is of no help. However, the big cat's staple diet is not coyote but deer, with lesser fare as available.

The cougar is sorely diminished in Canada. The British Columbia interior and Vancouver Island are the only regions where it still exists in any significant numbers. Large meat-eaters are always at the top of the big game hunter's most-wanted list, whether out of fear, resentment, envy, or greed is never entirely clear. What is clear is that the cougar has many attributes that attract merciless persecution: size, beauty, intelligence, and independence.

In the lowest valleys of the montane forest, pockets of native grassland support a community you would ordinarily expect to find far to the east in the southern prairie provinces. There are semi-arid places with prickly-pear cactus, sagebrush, antelope bush, rabbitbush, and bunch grasses. There are also sloughs which look like those on the prairies, complete with "puddle ducks" such

as mallard, shoveler, and widgeon.

There is one duck here, however, you will not ordinarily see on the prairies, and that is the cinnamon teal — small, dark burnt-red, and with a blue forewing. Like its much more widespread relative, the green-winged teal, it likes small water bodies with muddy shores and concealing vegetation. With the cinnamon teal's distribution being so limited, the British Columbia dry interior draws many birdwatchers on its account alone.

SUBALPINE FOREST

The subalpine forest occurs at high elevations from the Rocky Mountains in Alberta west through much of British Columbia. In extreme northern British Columbia and central Alberta, it blends into the continent-wide boreal zone, with which it has many affinities, the most obvious being conifers.

In the Rockies the subalpine forest ranges between elevations of about 1,300 to 2,200 metres. Typical trees are alpine fir, lodgepole, whitebark and limber pines, and Engelmann spruce. Where

it abuts the wet Columbia forest of the British Columbia interior its range is generally lower, extending from about 1,400 to 1,700 metres, again with a preponderance of Engelmann spruce, alpine fir, and whitebark pine, but with the addition of mountain hemlock and white spruce.

There is considerable animal activity in the subalpine forest during spring and fall. Birds and hoofed mammals migrate to and from the lush, open meadows which are scattered through these forests near timberline, and of course beyond.

One of the most conspicuous of these vertical migrants is the wapiti. Notable for its great size (the second largest deer after the moose) and its imperial bearing, this deer is one of the grand sights still common in the mountains. In spring these animals leave their winter quarters to move to higher, greener pastures, and by summer roam up to graze on the lush alpine meadows above treeline. As winter approaches, they make their way down into the valleys again.

Wapiti differ from mule deer and white-tailed deer, which are heavy browsers, in preferring to graze on grasses, sedges, and various flowering herbs. In winter they paw away the snow to reach the grass. When conditions are difficult — which happens when a severe winter coincides with an unusual population build-up — the wapiti sometimes resort to the bark of poplars and aspens. You can see stands of trees with black scars up to the height a wapiti can reach. Under conditions of extreme duress, wapiti even eat the needles of pines, Douglas-fir, and balsam fir. Such circumstances, however, are exceptional.

On the other hand, evergreens are important winter forage for mule deer which depend a great deal on Douglas-fir and cedar. Like the wapiti, they migrate up and down the mountainsides in

94

Mule Deer: Small herds of mule deer are common in the subalpine forest during summer when they graze in the lush meadows near timberline. Smell plays an important role in mule deer society. Specialized glands located between the lobes of the deer's hooves deposit scent as it walks. These scent trails help mule deer keep track of other herd members. Other glands, located in tufts of stiff hair on the inside of the hocks, are used to establish dominance. The tufts hold glandular secretions and urine which is carefully sprayed onto this area. To show it is subordinate and thereby avoid conflict, a deer sniffs the hocks of the more powerful animals it encounters.

Rocky Mountains: In the Athabasca Valley of Jasper National Park, the subalpine forest disappears when the terrain becomes too steep for soils to form. Exposure, elevation, climate, and slope are all factors which determine the limit of tree growth on a mountainside.

the course of the seasons. In summer some males reach the alpine meadows, but few females climb that high. In winter the mule deer also retire to the lower slopes that have the least snow cover.

Conditions in the subalpine region are a hardship for most tree species: extreme elevation, strong winds, and long, cold winters. Whitebark pine, however, can survive in the harshest of exposed places by the simple expedient of restricting its growth. From a medium-sized tree at lower levels, it shrinks to become little more than a shrub at the highest elevations, its long, twisted branches spreading flat over the ground. Whitebark pine provides food for the flashy, noisy flocks of Clark's nutcrackers which dote on the seeds they extract from its cones.

As might be expected from their conspicuous flocking behaviour and their perpetual noise-making, nutcrackers are related to the crows and jays. They are permanent residents of the mountain forests, but like the deer they usually move up and down with the changing seasons.

Campsites in the high country also attract one of the most beautiful small mammals, the golden-mantled ground squirrel. Looking somewhat like an over-size, brightly coloured chipmunk, this species frequents openings in the subalpine forest as well as areas above the treeline. Generally, it occurs between about 1,500 and 2,400 metres and nearly always in or around Engelmann spruce, Douglas-fir, and pines. From early September until the middle of April, it hibernates in a burrow, the entrance of which is skillfully concealed beneath some overhanging stump or rock ledge. During the summer it returns to its burrow every evening, venturing forth in the morning only after the chill is off the air. A network of trails is evident between burrows, criss-crossing one another in a

Clark's Nutcracker: Common birds of the subalpine forest, Clark's nutcrackers are intelligent and curious. They follow coyotes and deer and quickly gather to investigate campsites. Their feeding habits are resourceful and wide-ranging: they hunt on the ground for beetles and crickets, catch butterflies on the wing, hammer on trees in woodpecker fashion for grubs, pry seeds from pine cones, steal scraps from tents and cabins, and raid the nests of other birds to eat the eggs or young. They store seeds for use during the winter and early spring, finding up to 70 percent of them under the snow.

Golden-mantled Ground Squirrel: A beggar and thief at campsites, the golden-mantled ground squirrel makes its home in openings in the subalpine forest, especially where there are rock outcrops and fallen logs. It first appears above ground in mid-April, sometimes tunnelling to the surface through a foot of snow. For the next five months the ground squirrel eats, plays, sunbathes, mates, and rears a family. Near the end of summer it stuffs seeds, berries, grass, and clover into its big cheek pouches using both front paws, and carts the load off to stock the winter burrow. In early September it disappears underground until spring, spending more than half its life in hibernation. In winter it rolls into a ball with tail wrapped around its head and shoulders, its body temperature close to freezing for days at a time.

labyrinth to which only the local ground squirrels have the key.

In the subalpine forest the change of seasons can be quite jarring and vegetation must respond quickly. Among the tree species, the alpine larch is undoubtedly the most visibly affected by the seasons. Larches (which include the tamarack) are the only deciduous conifers in Canada. They lose their needles in the fall and grow new ones in the spring.

In the fall the alpine larch comes into its glory. The dying needles turn bright yellow, glowing in the autumn sun. This is a moment when the processes of life and season appear to be briefly suspended in time, as though the earth had stopped turning, and the sun had stopped circling for one precious instant of silent reflection. But the moment passes quickly and the world crashes into life again, as the hoarse whistling call of a rutting bull wapiti reverberates through the still, cold air of the mountain valley.

Wapiti: The bull wapiti must feed steadily to grow antlers and build up strength for the rutting season. In the fall the bull becomes irritable, rolling in urine-soaked wallows, bugling and sparring with other males. A dominant bull may gather a harem of 30 cows and calves.

Alpine Larches: In September the green foliage of alpine larch turns to gold, and before winter arrives the needles drop off. The larches, including the tamarack, are the only deciduous conifers in Canada.

Stone Mountain: The progression from forest to alpine tundra can be seen on Stone Mountain in the Yukon. Each zone contains distinctive plants and animals. Many animals — deer, bear, grouse, Dall's sheep — move up and down the mountain in response to seasonal change.

The Alpine

On every high mountain there is an elevation beyond which trees cannot grow. This is called the treeline and the region above it is the alpine zone. Even the hardiest trees eventually yield to either cold, fierce winds, dryness, thin soils, or a combination of these. Not all plant life ceases at the treeline; many of the most beautiful flowering species grow in the higher elevations of the alpine.

In western Canada the treeline generally increases in elevation from west to east across the mountain ranges, until in the Rockies it is found at about 2,200 metres. The treeline is rarely straight. Around an individual mountain, it will zig-zag unevenly as a result of the contour and exposure. Often, there are islands of trees well above the treeline just as there are many open patches in the forest below.

Above the treeline there may be gently rolling meadows with tundra plants reminiscent of the arctic, or steep cliffsides where nothing but the hardiest shrubs, a few grasses, and lichens can persist. In the alpine zone, contour and exposure govern the length and angle of sunlight, the extent of erosion, and the chilling and drying effect of the wind — all important factors in plant growth.

Winter distinguishes the true denizens of the alpine zone from the summer visitors. There are few options in the high country when October comes. You can migrate, like most of the birds. You can hibernate until spring returns, which is what some small mammals and all plants do. Or, most

THE ALPINE

challenging of all, you can tough it out like the mountain goats, remaining in the open as usual and moving around just enough to avoid inhospitable places during severe weather.

We should not think that the alpine zone is one great snowpack in winter. On the contrary, much of it is bare. The swirling winds keep large areas brushed almost clear of snow. Accumulations take place where physical barriers, acting like snow fences, cause it to pile up.

The winter of 1981-82 in Kluane National Park was very cold, even for the Yukon, and there was also a greater snowfall than usual. The winds were much reduced from normal and deep snow covered the vegetation, even on alpine ridges that were usually swept clear. As a result, the Dall's sheep could not feed as usual, and the population being studied at one mountain by biologists Douglas Burles and Manfred Hoefs fell by about 25

Dall's Sheep: A ewe and her lamb feed on grasses and herbs on an alpine ridge. After the lambs are born in late spring, older ewes lead flocks up to higher elevations to forage. Mature rams stay off by themselves until the breeding season in early winter when there is promiscuous mating and much head-butting among males. Rearing on their hind legs, the rams lunge at each other, crashing horns. The performance is mostly ritual and rarely does either animal get hurt.

percent (from 241 to 180). Older animals and young lambs were hardest hit.

The behaviour of Dall's sheep and the related bighorn, two of the most splendid animals of the high country, illustrates an important ecological principle. It is popular to think how brave these creatures are to endure such bleak and dreadful circumstances. But we forget that the sheep have not been driven into the alpine. They belong there. The cliffsides, rockslides, and outcroppings are the sheep's home and sanctuary from grizzlies, wolves, and cougars. To avoid these predators they head for the most precipitous, tumbled rockfalls where nothing but a rifle bullet can possibly follow.

Dall's and the related bighorn sheep move up and down with the seasons to some extent, and they have winter foraging ranges where they can get at food by pawing through a light snow cover. Mountain goats, on the other hand, tend to stay put year round. Their habitat is so extreme in places that it is difficult to see just what an individual animal is standing on; with no apparent underpinning it appears glued to a sheer rockface. Goats inhabit the steepest, roughest, and coldest terrain imaginable. Their split hooves are short and wide; around the outside rim there is a hard, horny shell; on the inside, a pad of soft, spongy material. These hooves resist slippage and take the impact of a jump without skidding. Goats can leap nonchalantly across a three metre chasm hundreds of metres deep. Here the howling winter wind is actually beneficial. Far from blowing the goats from their perches, it keeps forage uncovered and accessible.

During the summer mountain goats frequent the lush alpine meadows to feed on a variety of grasses, herbs, and woody plants. Occasionally deep winter snow forces them to abandon the high alpine for lower elevations where plant growth is more exposed. Here they graze on conifers and paw through the thin snows to reach lichens, mosses, and other plants. While wandering about looking for good grazing, many goats are killed or seriously crippled by avalanches and rock slides.

Few birds can live in the alpine zone year round, but the white-tailed ptarmigan does just that. It may move down into the forest below the treeline in the most difficult times, but normally it remains on wind-swept alpine meadows and rockslides. Here the wind does more for the ptarmigan than merely expose its food and grit. It piles the snow into banks which the birds use for shelter from the very wind that supplied it. There are few events in nature from which no one benefits.

Tombstone Mountains: This remote region of alpine tundra in the Yukon receives few visitors and is a haven for grizzlies, mountain goats, and Dall's sheep. The jagged peaks of the Tombstone Mountains, seen in the distance, rise 2100 metres.

Mountain Goat: Living in some of the roughest terrain in Canada, this member of the antelope family is the most skilled rock climber of all North American mammals. Equipped with short, muscular legs, non-skid soles, and flexible toes, mountain goats clamber about near vertical rock faces where few other animals venture. Such precipitous terrain is safe refuge from less agile predators.

Hoary Marmot: This grizzled marmot lives in alpine meadows where soil is deep enough to enable burrowing. Suitable habitat at alpine heights is limited, so marmots tend to congregate in the same area. There are always a few individuals on sentry duty atop boulders or rock tumbles with good visibility. On sighting anything suspicious, the sentry issues a piercing whistle, which is passed along the mountainside warning the colony to retreat underground. Grizzlies are perhaps most feared, being strong enough to dislodge large rocks and dig the marmots out of their burrows.

Ptarmigan have heavily feathered legs and feet, enabling them to snowshoe about on the drifts. Deep beneath that snow, especially if it covers a jumbly rockfall, are the winter tunnels and pathways of the pika. This strange, little animal, related to the rabbit, is common on rocky, landslide sites above the treeline. It is active all year, bustling about beneath the snow and between the rocks, nourished by a large haystack it has accumulated during the summer. Its gathering was not easy, for plant life is sparse in this stony region, and the pika is vulnerable to predators if it ventures beyond the protection of its boulders. Even when it hides,

it is not safe from the ermine which is small enough to pursue it directly into its subterranean domain.

The final winter option for animals is sleep, and of those that do so, by far the most noteworthy is the hoary marmot. This large, grizzled relative of the woodchuck hibernates for a good eight months of the year surviving on an exceptional build-up of fat reserves. Toward the end of summer its waddling gait suggests that if it swallowed one more morsel it would be unable to make it back to the burrow. Underground it is relatively safe, except occasionally from grizzly bears which, thanks to prodigious strength and fearsome claws, are

Alpine Stream: The steep slopes above timberline cause rapid run-off and water is often in short supply. The lushest growth of alpine plants occurs along stream banks and on gentler slopes where there is deeper soil and more moisture collecting from melting snow. Shown in the photograph are alpine arnica, red monkey flower, fleabane daisy, and yarrow.

Following Pages: These peaks near Maligne Lake in Jasper National Park are typical of the Rocky Mountains. The four adjoining national parks of Banff, Jasper, Kootenay, and Yoho form the largest mountain park area in the world, one that attracts millions of visitors each year. The steep slopes provide only scattered footholds for plants, and in some areas hikers unwittingly crush vegetation and cause erosion, leaving scars which sometimes take decades to heal.

Fly on Alpine Arnica: Attracted by colour and fragrance, a fly feeds on the nectar of alpine arnica. Alpine meadows are a magnet for many kinds of animals during the summer when plant production is at its peak.

adept at digging out marmots not sufficiently tunnelled in under heavy boulders.

Probably no habitat in the world, save the arctic, shows such a dramatic difference between winter and summer as does the alpine. When for so many months there was unrelenting wind and icy dreariness, the brief alpine summer is aglow with wildflowers, green grasses, and sedges and alive with birdsong. The rosy finches return from lower elevations to resume their rich, nuptial warbling on mountain summits. Pipits sprinkle tinkling flight songs over the meadows, and golden eagles silently soar past cliffsides. Ptarmigan throw together their sparse nests in natural depressions on the ground. Blue grouse strut and hoot through the meadows. Pikas emerge, perch on their rocky, front stoops, and begin their strange, ventriloquistic bleating. Marmots whistle piercingly from the rockslides, and the plain greyish-brown Brewer's sparrow jubilantly pours forth its long, pleasingly complicated song. The season of growth and reproduction is so compressed at these elevations that every week, every day — it seems every hour — is of incalculable value. A feeling of urgency permeates every living thing.

This is especially true of alpine plants which must complete their annual processes in a few critical weeks. Different plants have different methods. Some of the treeline conifers, having long since given up the battle to grow upright, propagate by layering. The tips of twigs touching the ground, should they find sufficient soil, will themselves produce roots and subsequent shoots. These are not new trees, merely extensions of the original, resulting in small clumps of genetically identical trees. Considering the brevity of the alpine summer, this process is more effective than

Blue Grouse: For the benefit of a nearby hen, a male blue grouse displays his orange eye combs and large, yellow neck sacs. Males often stand on a high spot and inflate their neck sacs to amplify the hooting which announces their presence to passing females. Unlike some other grouse, males of this species do not gather in groups during the breeding season.

112

gambling on a season favourable enough to produce cones and seeds. Even then germination of a conifer seed under such conditions would be a long shot.

Soil is not necessarily at a premium everywhere in alpine country. In areas on the gentler, protected slopes of the wetter ranges, there are dazzling stretches of blue, yellow, pink, white, and red meadows. Each plant species has its own way of surviving the harsh climate. Some carry downy insulation against cold and desiccation; some hug the ground; some have succulent leaves to conserve water; some huddle in dense clumps or cushions. All are exceedingly fast at leafing, flowering, and setting seed. Most alpine plants have very large flowers relative to the size of the rest of the plant, the better to attract early season insects for pollination.

Although many hikers are lured up to alpine heights by the beauty of the flowers, the colourful display is intended to impress not people but insects. Most flowers rely on insects, and sometimes birds, to achieve pollination. These airborne couriers are lured to the blooms from considerable distance by bright colours and enticing perfumes. Once they arrive, the flower treats them to a feast of nectar and pollen. While feeding, the insects bump into the stamens, knocking off pollen that adheres to their bodies and is later deposited, again unwittingly, on the pistil of another plant which results in fertilization.

The prevalence of yellow in many alpine blooms — cinquefoil, buttercup, glacier lily, wood betony, daisy, arnica — is an indication that this colour is highly visible to many insects. Red attracts hummingbirds. Bees favour blue, and it is interesting that access to the nectar reservoir of blue lupines can only be gained by a strong, heavy-bodied insect like the bumblebee.

Alpine soils become thinner, drier, and poorer with increasing elevation, slope, and exposure. Along with the grasses, sedges, and cushion plants, the heaths are well adapted to these demanding conditions. Two species of heath, red and white, are especially common, adding splashes of colour where few other flowering plants can grow. But even the heaths have their limit. Above them, aside from a thin smear of lichen on rock here and there, plant life ceases.

Wildflowers: In the few weeks of alpine summer, plants must not only develop flowers, seeds, and fruit, but store enough food in their roots to enable them to get a quick start the next spring. The blossoms of blue lupines, yellow alpine ragworts, and red monkey flowers absorb sunlight readily and are several degrees warmer than white-petalled species. This allows greater nectar production which in turn attracts more insects and leads to quicker pollination.

Least Chipmunk: A least chipmunk sniffs at a broadleaved lupine. Chipmunks don't eat flowers but feed on seeds, insects, and small berries. This smallest of western chipmunks cannot store enough fat to last through a winter of hibernation like many other alpine rodents. Instead it stores food in its burrow which it snacks on until spring. Theft of food caches by neighbouring chipmunks is common, and many chipmunks disperse their winter supply in smaller, scattered hoards away from the main burrow.

Moose: By mating season in the fall, the velvet covered knobs on this moose will develop into hard, bony antlers — enormous structures larger than those of any other member of the deer family. During the rut bulls hope to attract females by trotting about their territories, thrashing shrubs and small trees with their antlers, and rolling in mud wallows. Moose sometimes feed on sprouting grass, their long front legs causing them to graze on bent wrists.

The Boreal Forest

Aspens and Fireweed: Found throughout the boreal forest, trembling aspen is identified by its greyish-white bark and fluttering foliage. The nearly circular leaves are suspended on long, flexible stems, causing them to tremble in the slightest breeze. Aspens and fireweed are among the first plants to occupy areas disturbed by fire and clearing.

Splashing out of the shallow muskeg water, crashing through brittle shrubbery and tangles of dead spruce limbs, a startled moose makes a frightful racket. The sound is explosive, shattering. When the moose reaches firmer footing it will switch gears into a strange, trotting gait that looks for all the world like loose scaffolding swaying in the wind. Its extraordinarily long legs move like those of no other deer, appearing to pump straight up and down, but covering great chunks of ground nonetheless. Banking into a turn, the huge animal seems to defy gravity momentarily, then resumes its fascinating, awkward-elegant pace to vanish behind a stand of tamaracks. Silence falls again, punctuated at times by the *hic! three beers* whistle of an olive-sided flycatcher, the wheeze of a boreal chickadee, the quiet chuckle of a grey jay.

The boreal forest is moose country. Like the moose, this vast stretch of conifers occurs not only in North America but across northern Europe and Asia. In Canada the boreal forest extends from Newfoundland to the Yukon and British Columbia. In the north it is bounded by the arctic tundra and to the south by the aspen parkland of the prairies and the mixed forests of Ontario, Quebec, and the Maritimes. It is larger than all the other Canadian life zones combined.

The tree cover is not precisely the same intercontinentally, but it is characterized throughout by conifers mixed with birches and poplars. There is a sameness across the zone in its short growing season, poorly nourished, acidic soils, and cold, long winters.

Although the dark evergreen mantle looks superficially uniform across the country, it does vary. Everywhere, however, it is dominated by spruces, both black and white. In the Atlantic

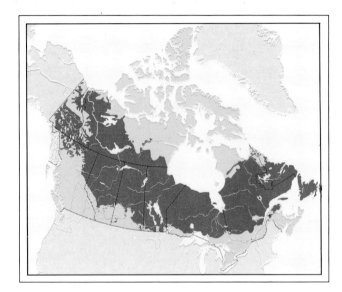

THE BOREAL FOREST

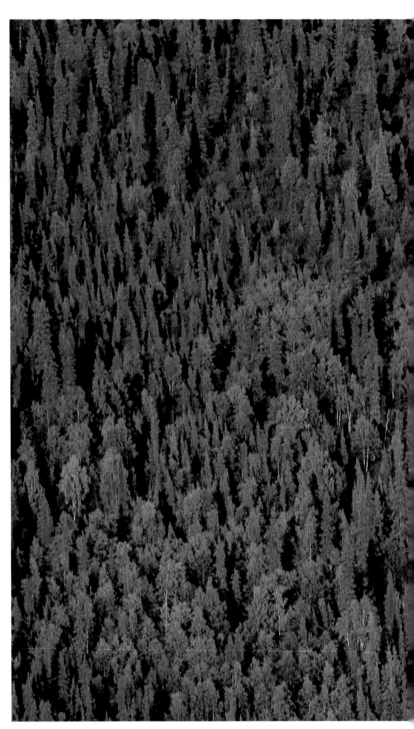

region red spruce is added, together with pines and white cedars, and some broadleaved species. Where it meets the Great Lakes-St. Lawrence forest, we find intrusions of beech, sugar maple, and hemlock. Across the northern prairies the boreal forest merges with aspen parkland and in the mountains with lodgepole pine and alpine fir, which are the replacements for the jack pine and balsam fir of the central and eastern parts. Tamarack grows throughout, except in the far northwest.

The single most characteristic feature of the boreal forest zone is muskeg. There are some 1,300,000 square kilometres of muskeg in Canada, much of it in the boreal forest. Muskeg is neither land nor water, but a mix of the two, like porridge or thin stew. The crust on a bowl of French onion soup best describes the surface. Wherever you stand, you stand in water. This is peatland, with

Boreal Forest: The boreal forest is the largest life zone in Canada. It stretches from Newfoundland to the Yukon and is dominated by a few cold-tolerant conifers: species of spruce, pine, fir, and larch. In open areas aspen, birch, and willow are common. The photo shows a forest near Dawson City of white spruce, alpine fir, aspen and birch. The rust-coloured spires occur when spruce becomes infested with beetles.

Willow Ptarmigan: Canada has three species of ptarmigan: the willow, rock, and white-tailed. All have feathered feet and legs and distinctive white wing quills. Ptarmigan have three different moults annually, and always seem to be exchanging feathers of one colour for new ones of another. The late summer plumage of this willow ptarmigan is beginning to show the first white feathers of winter.

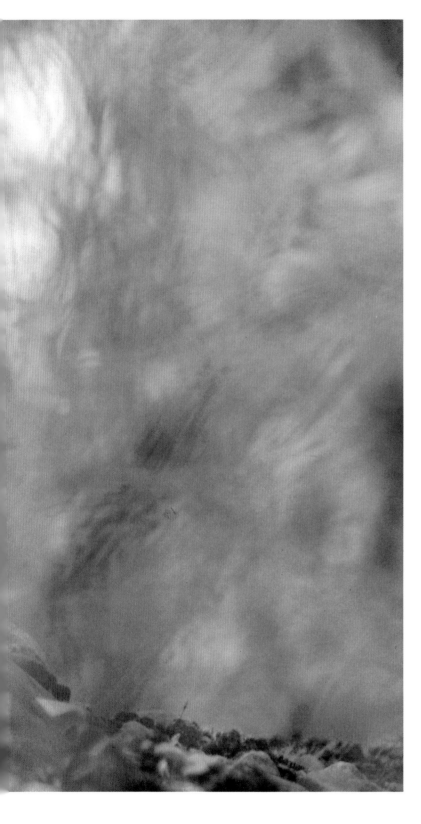

waterlogged, dead sphagnum mosses and other plant debris. There are plenty of living plants too, such as scrub willow and birch, leatherleaf, Labrador tea, sundew, pitcher plant, and cranberry — even various species of orchids, but only those which can tolerate the wet, highly acidic conditions. Of trees, black spruce grow best here, but these are often stunted and leaning "drunkenly" in their precarious, mushy footing. Muskeg must be visited in summer, if only for the authentic northern experience of braving hordes of blackflies and mosquitoes!

The boreal forest is stippled with thousands of small lakes, sloughs, and potholes occurring in depressions left behind by retreating glaciers. Wetland vegetation is vital to wildlife, providing both food and shelter for ducks and geese. In addition the cattails and bulrushes bordering the wetlands attract loons, grebes, and various songbirds, as well as muskrats and mink.

Nearly all the boreal birds migrate. Even those few species that remain in the north year round usually move a bit south, among them hawks, owls, jays, ravens, three-toed woodpeckers, grouse, ptarmigan, and a few others. Sometimes, however, there are enormous emigrations, known as irruptions, from the boreal forest.

Irruptions are caused by population explosions, resulting in movements that are sporadic, irregular, and usually without warning. Birdwatchers in southern Canada are familiar with "invasions" of boreal species from time to time. Such irruptions most often occur in the smaller birds such as finches (especially crossbills and siskins), chickadees, and waxwings, and they are sometimes accompanied by a much smaller number of their predators, such as northern shrikes.

Varying Hare: Named for its changes in coat colour — from brown-grey in summer to snow-white in mid-winter — the varying hare is found throughout most of Canada south of the northern tundra. In lush, brushy areas populations are as dense as 3,600 per square kilometre. Like other northern animals, its numbers fluctuate greatly over just a few years. Hares are known for their incredible reproductive potential: females may bear as many as four litters per year. They begin breeding in early spring, produce a litter five weeks later, and then remate within a few hours of giving birth. To shun a courting buck, females drum the ground with their large hind feet or leap into the air.

These irruptions seem to be related to the production of the birds' food. In one year, for example, there may be particularly favourable weather at nesting time, followed by an unusually good food crop in the fall. The result would be increased rates of survival over the following winter, the population rising above its normal level. But the chances of there being two favourable years in succession are slight. If the following year is a poor one, even an average one, the birds may find that their numbers have overshot the level of support that their range can sustain. Then they begin to move south, sometimes in astonishing numbers, in search of food.

Better understood are the cyclic fortunes of the snowshoe hare which thrives for periods of between six and thirteen years then experiences a population collapse. The numbers build up gradually until eventually the bush seems to be swarming with hares. Then suddenly and dramatically, the population collapses in a single season.

While the hares were on the upswing, things were never better for their predators —foxes, coyotes, weasels, bobcats and lynx, and the large owls. The sudden decline in hares, however, is not brought about by predation. Numbers of the preyed-upon govern numbers of predators, not the other way round.

The disappearance of the snowshoe hares affects their predators in different ways. Most of them simply turn to other fare. Lynx, on the other hand, follow a cyclic pattern that "echoes" that of the hare. Their numbers, as though by momentum, will peak after those of the hare, and their collapse is delayed. But it is equally dramatic. Much of the information on snowshoe hare and lynx cycles has been deduced from records of fluctuating prices for their pelts in the fur industry.

Both the hare and the lynx are striking examples of adaptation to northern conditions. The hare is well known for its large, wide hind feet which enable it to cope with almost any kind of snow cover. Less well known is that the lynx's feet are so broad and feathery that it distributes only about a third of the pressure on the snow as would a house cat one third its weight!

Snow conditions during the boreal forest winter are very important to the largest animals. In light, fluffy snow, even if it is fairly deep, the moose has little difficulty. Its long, high-stepping legs carry it along while any pursuing wolves flounder and become exhausted. If there is a crust, however, the wolves race along on top of it, while the moose crashes through at every step, often cutting its legs, and soon tiring. Deer have trouble with deep snow, and seek areas of light cover, or else tramp the snow down in sheltered "yards".

Lynx: Well adapted to the boreal forest, the lynx roams easily over deep snow on wide, padded paws. Although the lynx preys mainly on varying hare, it kills animals as large as deer and moose which are sometimes slowed down by snow conditions. The future well-being of the species is threatened by human settlement and clearing of forests. Each lynx requires a home range of 150 to 200 square kilometres, and thus large areas of wilderness are necessary to sustain a viable population.

Caribou: The distribution of caribou in the north varies from winter to winter. Often herds leave the tundra to feed in the shelter of the boreal forest where the snow cover is lighter. Caribou thrust their muzzles into the snow, locating plants by smell. They use their broad, concave hooves to clear small feeding patches. During the middle of the day, they move out of the trees to rest and chew their cuds in the open — on ridges or frozen lakes and rivers — where they are not vulnerable to surprise attacks by wolves.

Great Grey Owl: Often seen hunting from a low perch, the great grey owl relies on acute hearing and binocular vision to locate its prey. It can detect mice and voles under a seemingly soundproof, opaque blanket of snow. Plunging down on its prey with talons spread wide, it clamps lethally onto its victim. Small prey is swallowed whole, and large animals are sheared into chunks. A few hours after the owl has fed, the indigestible fur and bone are compacted in the stomach into golf ball size pellets and regurgitated.

Caribou are particularly well equipped for travelling in the changing boreal landscape. These animals always look big-footed for their size, but it is no accident, given their habitat. They are either slogging it out through muskeg in summer or negotiating icy surfaces in winter. Accordingly, the hooves change with the seasons. In summer the weight of the animal rests on large, soft pads which give it maximum contact with mushy ground. When the snow returns, the pads decrease in size, and the hard, horny edges of the hoof grow out, ideally suited for travelling on ice and packed snow. Their very large, splayed hooves are also a help in swimming, which caribou undertake without hesitation in the coldest water.

Winter is by no means threatening for most boreal animals. Snow provides a world of comfort and convenience for many of the smallest mammals. Voles, shrews, and some mice scurry about all winter in runways and through space between the ground and the bottom of the snow cover. If you look carefully, you can sometimes see their tiny breathing holes. The snow insulates them against the bitter cold above, hides them from the eyes of hawks and owls, and as long as they do not make too much noise, from the sharp ears of foxes and coyotes.

Another hunter of these small fry in the boreal forest is the great grey owl. Even though it is Canada's largest owl, the great grey appears to subsist largely on mice and voles. Although it may nest in conifers, the great grey often selects a poplar or aspen grove on a former burn. Usually the nest was constructed in another year by hawks or crows, but sometimes the owl finds a suitable platform where the top of a large tree has broken off. In either case it does little in the way of construction and does not line the nest. The eggs are laid at

intervals of from two to twelve days. But since incubation begins with the first one, the young also hatch at intervals, and the earliest arrivals are considerably larger than the last. In times of food shortage the oldest chicks may well devour the youngest. In the best years, however, all will make it, and owls have laid as many as nine eggs, as though to ensure against the inevitability of a poor season in the future.

The northern limit of the boreal forest marks the end of tree cover. We sometimes speak of the boreal and northern tundra zones as being separated by the treeline. But the treeline is by no means a line on a chart. Rather, it is an area of forest-tundra transition, a band often hundreds of kilometres wide. In many places the forest and tundra are quite evenly intermingled, and we can see "islands" of one surrounded by pure expanses of the other. Often you can look through the branches of large spruces out onto the open tundra, and in some places there are clumps of quite respectable spruces growing far from any other trees.

In other spots you can see dwarfed evergreens sprawling helter-skelter for kilometres.

The forest-tundra transition area is the land of cladonia lichen, also called reindeer moss. These lichens are the winter staple for the herds of caribou which in the fall move off the tundra and into the protection of the woods. This transition area is also habitat for some summer breeding birds. Smith's longspur nests along the northern edge of the diminishing spruces and on the adjacent tundra in a thin strip from the southwestern corner of Hudson Bay to the Beaufort Sea and along the north slope of the Yukon and Alaska. The large, handsome Harris' sparrow is another which nests only in the treeline band from Hudson Bay to the Mackenzie delta. The short-billed dowitcher, though not usually venturing out beyond the trees, likes the muskeg belt. Such species, neither of the forest nor of the tundra, enjoy the best of both these worlds.

Northern Boreal Forest: The northern extent of the boreal forest is marked by the arctic tundra, a region where normal tree growth is prevented by a cold, harsh climate and barren, rocky terrain. The transition between the boreal forest and the tundra is often gradual and indistinct, and in places is many kilometres wide.

Forest Floor: A banquet of fungi, bearberry, and lichens carpet the forest floor near Whitehorse in the Yukon. Fungi are important food for chipmunks and squirrels, bearberry fruits are eaten by grouse, and lichens are a mainstay of caribou.

Short-billed Dowitcher: This small shorebird nests in muskeg, bogs, or marshes in open areas of the boreal forest. Like other birds that live in wet habitats, it must preen regularly to keep its plumage well oiled to resist water.

127

The Northern Tundra

Tundra Ground Cover: Lichens, evergreen bearberry, and the scarlet leaves of dwarf blueberry cover a patch of autumn tundra.

Polar Bears: Polar bears wrestle on the frozen beach at Cape Merry near Churchill, Manitoba. Scores of bears gather here each fall waiting for the ice to form on Hudson Bay so they can roam out to hunt seals.

In the mainland Northwest Territories, the term "barrens" is synonymous with tundra. The first white adventurers who cast their eyes upon these frozen lands can be forgiven for finding them wanting. There is little drama in the flat topography, to be sure, and the landscape appears to be empty of everything but scattered rocks. Yet the tundra is not at all barren. It is covered by plant life of many kinds, including trees — granted not trees of the stature we know in the south. There is an abundance of exquisite wildflowers in spring and early summer, and there are many species of animals, among them some of the most beautiful and impressive in the world.

The arctic climate imposes severe limitations on all tundra life. And the most important limiting factor is the permafrost, ground that is frozen all year round. It can be gravel, soil, muck, bedrock, peat, or solid ice, so long as it doesn't thaw in the summer. In the high arctic permafrost can be several hundred metres thick. At its southern limit, shallow pockets are scattered deep into the boreal forest.

Permafrost is a good example of the delicate interrelationship between the life forms and climate of the northern tundra. Obviously no plant can grow in ice. If there are to be plants, and thus animals, then there must be an annual thaw on the surface long enough and deep enough to allow plant growth to proceed. At the same time, plants must have water. The permafrost must not thaw too deeply in spring, or the water would run off and be lost to the vegetation. So the underlying permafrost, which is not reached by the spring thaw, holds the water near the surface

129

Red-breasted Merganser:
Arctic wetlands are nesting grounds for many species of water birds, including red-breasted mergansers. Their nests are depressions on the ground lined with down and sometimes a few leaves. Usually they are located under a bush and near water to ensure a dependable food supply for the nesting season. Red-breasted mergansers feed on small fish and crustaceans. Sometimes a flock may string out and drive fish into shallow water where they are more easily caught.

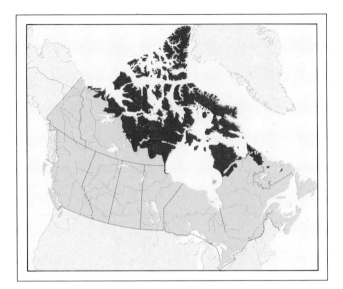

THE NORTHERN TUNDRA

where plant roots can get at it. In turn, vegetative cover insulates the ground from the summer sun, preventing the thaw from penetrating too deeply.

Water is very unevenly distributed in the far north. Much of the tundra is flat and when spring thaw begins, such snow cover as may have accumulated (precipitation is extremely light) tends to run off quickly to gather in shallow ponds. Water also collects in depressions and cavities caused by frost heaving and in poorly drained, low-lying meadows. Since the summers are generally cool, there is little evaporation; where there is a pond in the spring there is usually a pond in the fall.

Animals, especially birds, tend to congregate on the edges of lakes and ponds and along the banks of streams and rivers. Although some species are attracted to the dry tundra, usually the wetter it is and the more lush the vegetation, the greater the number of birds. Arctic wetlands are nesting grounds for loons, swans, geese, ducks, and shorebirds. A good three-quarters of arctic species are

130

Caribou: As well as being the most numerous large animal in the north, caribou support many other creatures — wolf, fox, raven, man. During summer their activity is dominated by efforts to avoid clouds of biting insects. They move into the wind, eating on the run, snatching mouthfuls of vegetation here and there. They crowd onto snowbanks, gravel bars, sand dunes, and windswept knolls and sometimes wade frantically into frigid water to escape. But the insects take their toll. During the peak of mosquito and blackfly season, one caribou may lose a litre of blood a week to insects.

water birds of one kind or another. Most of them are also found in the arctic regions of Europe and Asia.

Most of the mammals, too, are circumpolar, including wolves, polar bears, arctic foxes, lemmings, wolverines, ermines, and caribou. In the course of a year the large animals have to cover great distances between widely scattered breeding grounds and food sources.

The migrations of caribou are legendary, both for the numbers of animals involved and the distances they cover. Having spent the winter in the relative shelter of the forest-tundra transition region, the herds begin to move out onto the tundra in March and April. Triggered perhaps by the changing angle of the sun, perhaps also by the sense of urgency of the pregnant females, they head for traditional calving grounds, often several hundred kilometres to the north. They usually travel in single file in long lines, trampling the snow in well-marked corridors. On they press, across rivers and often through deep snow, heading unerringly toward the ground of their birth. From year to year the herds may take quite different routes. This protects the thin and vulnerable arctic vegetation because the animals feed, and necessarily trample, as they go. It also makes it difficult to predict the whereabouts of the herds. It is amazing how many caribou may be in an area without being visible. Then, as though by magic, they appear over a rise on the horizon, the long strings doggedly moving toward their distant goal.

Why do the animals undertake such long and perilous treks to the north when one piece of open tundra would seem as appropriate as any other for bearing calves? George Calef, a caribou authority, has suggested three possible reasons. One is that wolves, the young caribou's major predators, have had to leave the herds they were following in order to den up and have their pups. This usually happens well before the caribou reach their calving grounds. Also, on these more northern and often upland areas, the biting flies have not yet emerged at calving time, and the newborn caribou have a chance to grow and strengthen before the summer insect onslaught. Finally, the more northerly calving places are less likely to receive the devastating sleet and freezing rain that occurs farther south.

During the summer caribou supplement their staple diet of lichens with sedges and grasses, various annuals, some small fruits, and the fresh, young twigs and leaves of arctic birches and willows. The latter are ground-hugging and dwarfed versions of the birches and willows we know in the south. To avoid the desiccating and chilling winds, some of these arctic species are completely prostrate with moss insulating the larger branches. Many of the herbaceous plants are covered with down, grow in tight clusters, or crouch in the lee of a bank, boulder, or grass hummock.

Arctic plants persist in the most improbable places. Wherever there is the slightest shelter and the merest accumulation of soil, there will be a diminutive, flowering wisp to celebrate the arctic summer.

Among the more successful colonizing plants are the grasses, thanks to light seeds that can travel great distances. Tundra grasses are the mainstay for Arctic ground squirrels and lemmings, themselves the mainstay for a long list of predators. When the lemmings are at the peak of one of their well-known population cycles, it is a bonanza for predatory birds, particularly jaegers, gulls, hawks, and owls. Among the mammals, ermines, wolves, foxes, and sometimes grizzly bears feast on lemmings. Even caribou have been known to partake. But when the lemming numbers are down, their predators must find alternative food, often by moving elsewhere. Snowy owls, for example, seem to turn up in southern Canada approximately every four years, a result, it is believed, of the lemming decline.

Northern tundra cycles are not well understood. The one thing we do know is that they are uneven. Also, weather in the arctic has a way of changing suddenly and without warning. A severe storm in early June can play havoc with the year's caribou calves, and with nesting tundra birds such as longspurs, sandpipers, and plovers. The summer season is so brief that many birds cannot nest again until the following year if the first effort is wiped out by a storm. Farther south, immediate renesting is common.

There may be long-term climate cycles in the far north that we will some day understand. We do know that all arctic plants and animals are geared to cope with the unexpected, and in spite of the extremes of the environment, they persist. The muskox exemplifies this. During the howling arctic winter, with its extreme wind-chill, a lone bull muskox stands there and endures. Thanks to his superlative under-wool, shaggy windbreaker, and specialized metabolic processes, chances are he will survive. Stoically standing, impassive in the terrible winter blizzard, he abides.

ARCTIC COAST

The Arctic coast supports much wildlife, although many of the species are equally dependent on the tundra or marine environments for survival. Barrenground grizzlies, bleached blond in the summer sun, patrol the beaches from time to time, feasting on the eggs of such seabirds as gulls, terns,

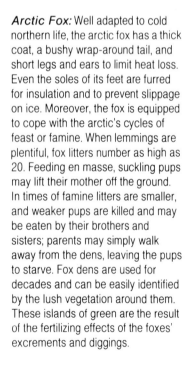

Arctic Fox: Well adapted to cold northern life, the arctic fox has a thick coat, a bushy wrap-around tail, and short legs and ears to limit heat loss. Even the soles of its feet are furred for insulation and to prevent slippage on ice. Moreover, the fox is equipped to cope with the arctic's cycles of feast or famine. When lemmings are plentiful, fox litters number as high as 20. Feeding en masse, suckling pups may lift their mother off the ground. In times of famine litters are smaller, and weaker pups are killed and may be eaten by their brothers and sisters; parents may simply walk away from the dens, leaving the pups to starve. Fox dens are used for decades and can be easily identified by the lush vegetation around them. These islands of green are the result of the fertilizing effects of the foxes' excrements and diggings.

Rocks: Much of Canada's north is characterized by barren landscape strewn with rocks. It is an indication of how little time, in geological terms, has passed since the last glaciers withdrew from these areas. Before plants can become established, soil must form, and in many parts of the arctic this process is still in its initial stages.

and eiders. The birds' eggs are products solely of the sea, but they feed the big terrestrial mammals. A snowy owl nesting far inland on the dry hummock tundra may explore the pebble beach on the chance of finding some incapacitated seaduck. Yellow-billed, red-throated, and Pacific loons nesting on inland tundra lakes and ponds travel to the coast to feed; the fishes and large invertebrates which sustain them are themselves sustained by the marine productivity of the Arctic Ocean. Do the loons belong to the tundra, the coastal, or the marine community?

The coast of the Beaufort Sea in the western arctic is one of the richest and most complex habitats in the north, harbouring elements of both terrestrial and marine communities, as well as some features of its own. Over the millions of years of geological process, this coast has been shaped by ice, by storms, and by meltwater. Today it is composed of a series of barrier beaches, braided gravel river deltas, spits, lagoons, gravel bars, and offshore islands. It is prime nesting habitat for many

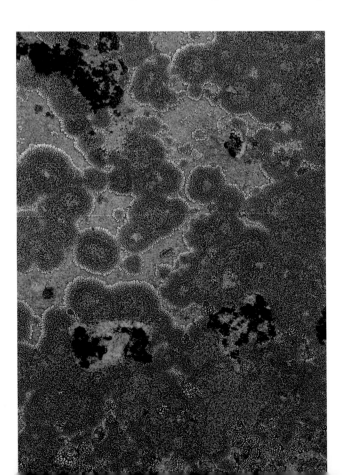

Lichens: The first plants to appear on tundra rocks are lichens. They produce an acid that over many years eats into rock. Weathering by frost, wind, and rain assists the process of breaking down the rock into tiny bits which combine with decayed plant matter to form soil. Arctic lichens grow very slowly. Crustose lichens, such as those shown in the photograph, form thin crusts on rocks. Some species grow only about one tenth of a millimetre per year, but they live for a very long time — some patches in the far north are several thousand years old.

Hudson Bay Shoreline: Winter's first snow accentuates the rocks and sand beach of Hudson Bay near Churchill. Although covering thousands of square kilometres, Hudson Bay is relatively shallow. The land rises at the rate of half a centimetre a year, steadily exposing more of the shoreline. The northern coastal area supports brushy aspen, willow, and dwarf birch with a ground cover of grass, lichen, and moss. The western coastal lowlands are breeding habitat for ducks, snow geese, tundra swans, snowy owls, gulls, terns, and many species of shorebirds. Polar bears, arctic foxes, red foxes, and wolverines patrol for dead whales, seals, and other carrion that may wash ashore.

137

Arctic Storm: High winds can drive ice into bays and channels, trapping whales and preventing sea birds from resting and feeding in the shallow water. Here a late autumn storm batters Cape Churchill on Hudson Bay.

species of birds, as well as a refuge for ducks in their late summer, flightless moult. The region provides a cornucopia of food, and a flyway for migrants in the fall.

Nunaluk Spit, at the mouth of the Malcolm River on the Yukon coast, is used both as a corridor and a stopover by literally millions of birds, including loons, swans, geese, ducks, hawks, eagles, falcons, cranes, plovers, sandpipers, dowitchers, jaegers, gulls, guillemots, owls, ravens, and assorted songbirds. On drier coastal tundra, large flocks of snow geese gather from their breeding areas to feed and fuel up for their fall departure south through the Mackenzie Valley. In the spring, no such leisurely pace was possible. They came north in their huge flocks as fast as their wings could carry them, and set about nesting immediately. Pairs were already formed; there was no time for courtship. Females were ready to lay the moment they arrived.

As on the tundra, coastal and marine communities are tied inexorably to the weather, but here it is the presence of sea ice, rather than permafrost

that is often critical. Although records are still too meagre to establish firm trends, examples have been documented of ice-related wildlife disasters. Migrating sea ducks, such as the king eiders that winter in the Bering Sea, arrive along the Beaufort coast in spring at a time when there are normally long cracks of open water in the ice (called leads) on which they can set down to rest and possibly feed. One year about 100,000 birds (10 percent of their population) died of starvation and exposure because the open water did not appear.

Another year, ice in Lancaster Sound in the eastern high arctic caused a critical delay in the nesting cycle of the immense colony of murres on Cobourg Island. The ice did not move out and the nesting birds were shut off from their food supply for three weeks, causing enormous mortality of young. No doubt occasional catastrophes have long been part of the natural history of certain arctic species. Fortunately their breeding potential seems sufficient for them to recoup, given the opportunity.

Just as a late spring breakup can wreak tremendous damage on birds, an early freeze in the autumn can also threaten wildlife. There are accounts of beluga whales being trapped in bays and lagoons by a sudden build-up of ice. In spite of being able to submerge for up to 20 minutes, the whales apparently are unwilling to swim for any distance under the ice, even if it is a matter of life and death. One group, cut off from the open sea unexpectedly, watched the ice encircle them until their vital access to air was shut off completely.

Polar bears have been observed attempting to catch belugas when they stray into shallow water along the coast, and have been recorded attacking them from ice floes. All arctic predators are opportunists. Although most of their food consists of

Snowy Owls: Well protected from the arctic cold, the snowy owl is blanketed by thick down and feathers extending over most of the bill and to the tips of the toes. Although not the largest, it is the heaviest of Canada's owls. As with many arctic animals, the snowy owl's activities are influenced by the lemming. In years when lemmings are plentiful, owls lay large clutches of eggs (as many as 14) and rear most of the young to flight stage. When the lemming population crashes (about every four years), many of the owls move into southern Canada where they are seen in open meadows or stubble fields hunting voles.

Polar Bear and Cubs: For the next two years this trio will roam over the ice pack in search of ringed seals. The mother will teach the cubs to sniff out a seal's lair concealed under the snow, and then to approach silently and pounce crashing through the snow onto the surprised prey. The cubs will watch her snatch seals from their breathing holes in the ice. Together they will feed on the dead carcasses of whales and raid seabird colonies for eggs. When the cubs are almost full grown, the family will split up. Aside from lack of food, the biggest threat to the cubs is man. Although hunting polar bears has been restricted since 1965 by international agreement, and their numbers have recovered, hundreds of bears are still killed each year.

ringed and bearded seals, polar bears also dine on bird eggs, wolf kills, or other carrion which they chance upon. They even eat small amounts of vegetable food, including berries and grasses of various kinds.

Polar bears are usually found wherever there are cracks and openings in the ice —likely habitat for seals. In the warmer weather, when the ice recedes from the coast toward the polar cap, many come ashore. Pregnant females bear their young in winter dens often many kilometres inland. Usually twin cubs are born. They suckle for a long time, up to and even beyond two years of age. On the summer ice you can sometimes see a female accompanied by two cubs, presumably males, that are bigger than she is.

The biological richness and abundance of certain areas of the Arctic Ocean are phenomenal. As in all marine communities, the food chain starts with the phytoplankton which is transformed by natural alchemy into thousands of other forms: algae, tiny crustaceans, clams and mussels, sea cucumbers and urchins, little codfish, bigger codfish, seals and walruses, bears and whales. The barren and inhospitable arctic is a fiction. Look at any roly-poly polar bear cub.

Sandhill Crane: In early spring flocks of sandhill cranes arrive over the prairies landing in a marsh or stubble field to rest and feed. There courtship takes place. The lanky cranes spring upward on spread wings, their gurgling cries floating across the flat land. Some cranes remain to nest on the prairies, but many continue northward to rear their young on tundra marshes and muskeg.

The Grasslands

Black-eyed Susan: The prairie is covered not only with grasses, but broadleaved herbs that produce large, colourful flowers. The bristly stems and hairy leaves of black-eyed Susan reduce evaporation, a necessary adaptation to the dry conditions of the grasslands.

The prairie stereotype is one of billiard-table flatness, a band of golden wheat at the bottom and a band of blue sky at the top. What the picture postcards cannot capture, of course, are the sounds of the grasslands. There is the gentle, light jingling of Sprague's pipit, the sweet, clear warbling of McCown's longspur, the soft, attractive notes of the chestnut-collared longspur. In brushy areas there is the loud, zippy chanting of the lazuli bunting, and where there is a scattering of trees, the truncated warbling of a mountain bluebird. And in season there is the rich, gurgling chorus of migrating sandhill cranes and the melancholy cries of geese at high altitude. All these sounds are woven in a delicate and intricate composition carried by the gentle, prairie breezes.

Prairie is usually defined as flat, or gently rolling, open grassland. At one time that was a valid description of an enormous portion of central North America. Today most of it is under cultivation for cereal crops, with the drier, more westerly areas used as range or pastureland. What is left of the prairie are pockets of the original ground cover, together with some of their natural inhabitants. In spite of massive "sod busting" over the years, there remain enough samples of pre-farming conditions to offer some taste of what must once have been.

There is another prairie world beneath the turf. It is the world of the diggers and burrowers, the tunnellers and maze-makers. In addition to the badgers, there are mice and voles, pocket mice and pocket gophers, owls and snakes, to say nothing of Franklin's and Richardson's ground

143

Coyote: On the Alberta prairie, a coyote leaps after a small rodent. Scenes such as this were common on the grasslands before European settlement. It is believed that this ocean of grass once supported 45,000,000 bison, the continent's largest land animal. There were nearly as many pronghorn, as well as mule deer, white-tailed deer, and wapiti roaming the unfenced plains. These herds were followed by predators — packs of wolves, grizzlies, coyotes, various fox species, bobcats, and cougars.

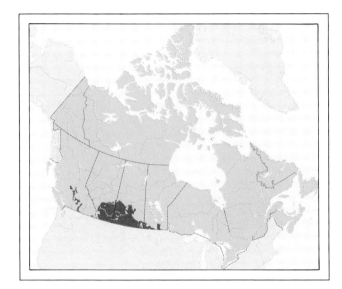

THE GRASSLANDS

squirrels. The former are more common at the edges of woods and in aspen parkland country. Richardson's, on the other hand, are at home on the open prairie, especially where soils are loose and easy to dig.

The Richardson's ground squirrel is the common "gopher" of prairie vernacular, and it occurs almost everywhere. If the number of these small mammals we see while driving the back roads is any indication, their total population must be phenomenal. Also difficult to imagine is the intricacy of their subterranean labyrinths of galleries and tunnels. In some of these chambers are stores of food that in many parts of the prairie turn out to be oats or wheat. For this habit, as well as for the custom of helping themselves to newly planted seed, nipping off shoots in the spring, and reaping ripened grain in the fall, Richardson's ground

squirrels are considered one of the most disreputable of farm pests. Of course it all depends on who is the beholder. Richardson's ground squirrels are seen in an entirely different light by weasels, foxes and coyotes, and soaring hawks and falcons, all of which have been unrelentingly persecuted by farmers while their erstwhile prey prospered.

At one time ponds, sloughs, potholes, and "kettles" of every size left by the glaciers and Lake Agassiz stippled the prairie landscape like stars in the night sky. Every depression, however slight, had its water. Today only a fraction of these remain.

It may be that no community is so rich and diverse, and seethingly active as that of a fresh water pond — from planktonic organisms through insect larvae, amphibians in various stages, and small fishes, to grebes, ducks, coots, and muskrats, to say nothing of the array of plantlife, on and under the water and at its edge. A prairie pond is a world in miniature.

The action begins at the bottom, with nutrient-rich muck from the decomposition of generations of cattails, sedges, and other aquatic plants. This is the "culture" from which arises an astounding volume and variety of animal life. If we had to pick one item of particular importance, it might well be the larvae of midges, the tiny flying insects that drift in smokelike masses over the still surface of a pond for the benefit of hawking swallows. In their aquatic stage they are minute, wriggling, wormlike creatures, fed upon in the millions by other aquatic larvae such as those of dragonflies and caddisflies. They are eaten also by those who come down from the surface to forage, such as ruddy ducks.

The male ruddy duck in breeding plumage seems to epitomize all the colour, verve, and vi-

vacity of the prairie pothole. His spring courtship ritual consists of erecting his fanlike tail, puffing out his chest and pressing his blue bill against it, and then emitting an explosive splutter as he rapidly vibrates his bill against his chest. As often as not this has the desired effect, and a nest will be carefully hidden in the emergent vegetation at the pond's edge. Other ducks, such as the mallard and pintail, prefer to nest in concealing grasses farther away from the water. Grebes build nests which actually float on the water's surface, anchored to standing vegetation and often well camouflaged.

The western grebe, the largest and most elegant of the family, chooses fairly large bodies of water with extensive marshes. Its breeding habitat must have plenty of emergent vegetation to hide the nest and stretches of open, deeper water for hunting small fishes. Peace and quiet are essential for its elaborate mating performance, a ritual as controlled, stately, and moving as a classical ballet.

Two grebes approach one another, raise their heads and present their bills. Ceremoniously and

Pintail Drake: Launching itself from a prairie slough, a pintail drake strikes the water with powerful wings and spread webs. Dabbling ducks, such as the pintail, can take off almost vertically in a blink of an eye, a manoeuvre that helps them evade falcons, hawks, foxes, and coyotes. Waterfowl suffer from hunting, accidental injestion of poisonous lead shot that hunters have discharged into wetlands, and loss of feeding and breeding habitat to agricultural and urban development.

Ruddy Duck: The ruddy duck nests where it can find water with bulrushes, cattails, or phragmites for cover. Here the drake courts the drab coloured hen. At the peak of his exuberant display, with tail feathers cocked forward and wings arched, he rattles a sky blue bill against his puffed up breast. For one of North America's smallest ducks (weight about 500 grams), the ruddy duck lays enormous eggs — slightly bigger than those of a great blue heron. While the female incubates a clutch of 10 or more eggs, the drake remains close by ready to escort the ducklings about the pond once they hatch, unusual behaviour for a male duck.

147

deliberately, they cross and recross their bills. Then, the two birds "stand" bolt upright on the water. With their necks and bodies stiffly erect and bills directly ahead, they move over the surface as though propelled by invisible motors. The dance ends as abruptly as it began, with both birds resuming a normal swimming posture as though nothing had happened. The courtship progresses for several weeks in this way, the dance often being resumed suddenly and without signal.

The extensive fresh water areas and cattail marshes also attract dense colonies of yellow-headed blackbirds. The males, with their striking yellow, black, and white plumage and strident voices, are unmistakable. Females are more modestly coloured in streaks of browns, but they show enough yellow on the throat to distinguish them from female red-winged blackbirds. Unlike the red-wings, the yellow-heads are normally polygamous. Several females build their nests within the larger home space of one male. The two blackbirds also differ in that the red-wing readily substitutes brushland, and even forest edge, for marshland as nesting habitat, whereas the yellow-head insists on good-sized water bodies with marsh vegetation, usually cattails.

Away from the lakes and sloughs in the grassland itself, are two noisy shorebirds which capture the attention of most naturalists — the long-billed curlew and the marbled godwit. Both are large, both brown with a pinkish cast, and both are seen farther from the water than most of their kind. The curlew (down-curved bill) and the godwit (upturned bill) are members of the sandpiper family, and both are bigger and more conspicuous than most of their relatives. Both symbolize the prairie grassland in its natural, uncultivated state.

DRYLANDS

Well after darkness has fallen on the dry plains and sandhills — and not even then if there is bright moonlight — a small form may appear and dash in great leaps across the open areas between

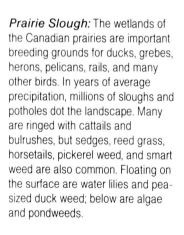

Prairie Slough: The wetlands of the Canadian prairies are important breeding grounds for ducks, grebes, herons, pelicans, rails, and many other birds. In years of average precipitation, millions of sloughs and potholes dot the landscape. Many are ringed with cattails and bulrushes, but sedges, reed grass, horsetails, pickerel weed, and smart weed are also common. Floating on the surface are water lilies and pea-sized duck weed; below are algae and pondweeds.

Western Grebe: Like all grebes, the western is an aquatic specialist. It has short, powerful legs mounted far to the rear like the tail fin of a fish, and long, lobed toes to grab the water. The grebe has short, stubby wings and takes off like an overloaded seaplane, running laboriously across the surface to build up speed for lift-off. Once airborne, flight is swift and straight, and the grebe must keep flying until it reaches water again. Should it come down on land in error or emergency, it can only sprawl along awkwardly on its breast, unable to take off again. In the 19th century thousands of western grebes were slaughtered by plume hunters who sold their skins to garment makers for five cents each. Today they are protected, but their former breeding habitat is much reduced and diminishing steadily.

the shrubbery. Like a miniature kangaroo, its strong hind legs propel it in bounds of up to two metres, a considerable accomplishment for a mammal little more than 27 centimetres long, half of which consists of a slender, elegantly tufted tail. This is Ord's kangaroo rat, an animal which more commonly lives far to the south in the arid zone of the western United States and central Mexico. Its presence had long been suspected in the near-desert of open brushland on the southern Canadian prairies, and was eventually confirmed in 1956.

The kangaroo rat lives in the region of short-grass prairie of which parts are rolling sand dunes, and other parts are covered by sagebrush and cactus with a thin scattering of blue grama grasses. It lies within the Palliser Triangle, an area which in 1857 was declared by explorer John Palliser as unfit for agriculture. Actually, only the most southern parts turned out to be so, modern agricultural methods having subjugated the greater part of it over the years. There is only a narrow strip along the United States border that remains in a natural condition.

Nowadays wildlife on the plains, sandhills, and coulees of the shortgrass prairie region seems sparse indeed. There are always the sounds of birds, of course, and evidence of burrowers and tunnellers of various sorts, but large mammals are rarely seen. The plains grizzly is gone and so are the wolves and great herds of bison. The 30,000 or so pronghorns that remain in Alberta and Saskatchewan are a tiny fraction of the original herds.

Although the white-tailed jack rabbit and the coyote are famous for their speed, there is no North American mammal as fleet as the pronghorn. It reaches speeds over short distances approaching 100 kilometres per hour, and it can

Pronghorn Antelope: Standing not much taller than a large dog and weighing about 45 kilograms, the pronghorn antelope is one of North America's smallest hoofed mammals. Its eyes, however, are larger than a horse's. On the treeless plains it can spot its chief predator, the coyote, several kilometres away. Individuals pass warning signals to other herd members by raising the long, white hairs that encircle their rump. The pronghorn's safety depends on speed, and its special anatomical features make it the fleetest land animal in North America. It has slim legs and compact hooves to quicken its stride, and highly flexible back and shoulder bones for maximum stride length. The pronghorn's big running muscles are grouped close to the body axis to maintain balance; and its heart, lungs, and windpipe are relatively larger than those of other hoofed mammals.

151

Pincushion Cactus: One of the pronghorn's foods is the soft berries of pincushion cactus which it somehow plucks from between the spines without injury. Like other cacti, this species has swollen, succulent stems and leaves that are modified into spines. In the absence of normal leaves, photosynthesis takes place in the fleshy stems. The blooms appear in July adding surprising spots of colour to the hot, dry, grey-brown landscape of the shortgrass plains.

Prairie Falcon: One of the swiftest birds of prey, the prairie falcon has a stream-lined torso with a thick, short neck and powerful shoulders. Propelled by rapid, shallow strokes of its pointed wings, the falcon overtakes its prey easily, usually feeding on ground squirrels but taking birds as well. It dives on large birds from above, knocking them to the ground with a talon blow. Smaller prey it simply plucks out of the air.

cruise at half that speed almost indefinitely. On the flatlands you can spot pronghorns from a considerable distance especially if they are running and flashing their white rump patches, a signal of danger.

Glimpses of other wildlife are usually much more brief. One may have only a few seconds, for example, to witness the stoop of a prairie falcon at a teal flying over an alkaline pond. The prairie falcon is the peregrine of the drylands — husky, powerful, the size of a crow, sandy coloured, and with black "armpits" and flanks. In its power dive at a flying target, its speed is difficult to judge, but the closely related peregrine has been timed at speeds up to 290 kilometres per hour. The prairie falcon usually knocks its prey out of the air with the force of its impact, either killing it outright with a talon blow, or disposing of it on the ground.

ASPEN PARKLAND

Although trembling aspens grow from the Yukon and British Columbia to Newfoundland, the term aspen parkland is usually applied to the belt that runs between the northern edges of the open grassland and the southern fringes of the boreal forest. To the north the aspens encounter spruces, pines, firs, and tamaracks mixed in with birches and others. To the south the aspen woodlands dwindle as pure grassland takes over.

The original ground cover in the aspen parkland consisted mainly of fescues or bunch grasses. There are few areas where these handsome grasses can be found today. Undisturbed individual hummocks, which may be the size of a bushel basket, form the basis for one of the richest assortment of plants on the prairies. Pasque flowers, lilies, roses, cinquefoil, and snowberry are found where openings in the aspen woodland permit. However, large

Peace River Parklands:
Grassland and aspen groves cover
the benches and bluffs of the Peace
River Valley in British Columbia.
Parkland habitat is a transition zone
between the southern grasslands
and the northern boreal forest.

154

tracts of such communities are becoming increasingly rare.

We often see groves of aspen in the middle of open land. Such groves get started in the same way other poplars do — from seeds riding on the wind. This process often begins with the burrowing activity of a ground squirrel, gopher, or badger. Loose earth left lying around provides a bed in which some wind-blown aspen seed can make a start. And it only takes one; new trees will follow by suckering. Other plants are dispersed in a similar way. The seeds of snowberry and prairie rose, once eaten by a bird, may be spread in its droppings, perhaps by a sharp-tailed grouse taking

Prickly Rose Thorn: The stems of prickly rose are armed with stiff thorns which protect the shrubs from trampling or browsing. The fleshy exterior of the fruits and the hairy seeds are valuable wildlife food. Thickets of wild roses are excellent nesting areas for birds and protective cover for many small mammals. Prickly rose is especially abundant in Alberta where it grows on hillsides, ravines, coulees, and in aspen woodlands.

its dust bath on an open patch of ground churned up by a gopher.

Sharp-tails are strongly governed by tradition. In the spring they congregate at special dancing grounds that have been used by their ancestors for generations. At the crack of dawn, the males begin their performance. The females watch. If anyone has ever wondered about the origin of some of the dances of the Plains Indians, one need only see a sharp-tail ceremony. With heads lowered, wings stretched out almost horizontally, and tail feathers erect, the male grouse execute a series of rapid stamping, shuffling patterns that look for all the world like an Indian dance in miniature. At the same time, by inflating purple sacs on the sides of the neck, the birds produce a low, cooing sound accompanied by a rattling of the tail feathers. The mechanics producing the sound are like those of a bagpipe, although some of us find the result somewhat more attractive.

Most of the badgers in Canada are now restricted to areas where farm machinery cannot go and so the edges and openings of the aspen woodland have become prime habitat. Badgers are weasels, which means they are carnivores. They live largely on ground squirrels and other small mammals, as well as the eggs and nestlings of ground-nesting birds, and some insects. They are formidable diggers. With their heavy forelegs and fearsome claws, they churn up the ground like trenching machines.

A good deal of the badger's excavating activity is devoted to the pursuit of the thirteen-lined ground squirrel, so named for the stripes on its back. This small and defenceless creature has developed some interesting techniques to foil the badger. It takes great pains not to leave any traces of loose dirt around the entrance to its burrow, and it even goes so far as to build an abrupt elbow in its tunnel — the badger digging in hot pursuit finds it difficult to throw earth out of a curved excavation. However, the squirrel has to go above ground to feed, and at such times is highly vulnerable to hawks, foxes, and coyotes, to say nothing of badgers.

Few life forms restrict themselves to aspen country; most range into the prairie or deeper into woodlands to the north. Still, it is difficult to think of an aspen grove without imagining a great horned owl dozing through the daylight hours in deep, leafy cover. Horned owls range throughout all of Canada south of the tundra. The owls of grasslands and aspen parkland are noticeably paler in colour than those elsewhere, and they often have a good deal of white in their plumage. Although this is not our largest owl — the snowy owl is about the same size and the great grey even larger — it is unquestionably the most powerful. Its diet includes animals as large as grouse, ducks, rabbits, and skunks. There are even accounts of it attacking house cats and porcupines. Occasionally it manages to catch its sworn enemy and dedicated disturber of its peaceful daytime rest — the ubiquitous crow. When a horned owl eats crow, it is apologizing for nothing!

Qu'Appelle Valley: The slopes of the Qu'Appelle Valley in southern Saskatchewan are forested with aspens, birch, and Manitoba maple. This broad, tranquil river valley is rich agricultural land and is well known for the berries that grow along the moist, north-facing slopes.

Carolinian Forest: Occupying the smallest area in the eastern forests zone, the Carolinian forest of southwestern Ontario has flora and fauna found nowhere else in Canada. These woods contain many trees normally associated with regions further south — Kentucky coffee tree, pawpaw, tulip-tree, sassafras, sycamore, chinquapin oak and, shown in the photograph, shagbark hickory.

The Eastern Forests

Pileated Woodpecker: A young pileated woodpecker calls out to its parent. Woodpeckers are well equipped for chopping into tree trunks to find insects and grubs. Their skulls are thick and the brains are protected by a thin cushion of shock-absorbing air. Woodpeckers have huge neck muscles, flint-hard bills, and long tongues coated with sticky saliva and fringed at the tip with barbs for snagging grubs and insects or licking up sap.

A loud *kukk-kukk-kukkuk* announces the approach of a pileated woodpecker flashing black, white, and red. Its sweeping wingstrokes carry it purposefully across an opening in the deciduous woods. As big as a crow, the pileated is by far the largest woodpecker in Canada and by all odds the most spectacular. Its large, oval diggings in apparently healthy trees are a sure sign of insects within. Braced with tail against a tree trunk, it delivers blows powerful enough to set large chunks of wood flying, even in hardwoods like beech and sugar maple.

Although widespread continentally, the pileated is especially characteristic of the Carolinian forest, the most southern and restricted region of the great spread of Canada's eastern forests. This narrow belt of deciduous hardwood trees tucked into the area bounded by Lakes Huron, Erie, and Ontario is an extension of the broadleaved forest that extends over much of the eastern United States. For the early European travellers, this area drew much the same astonishment as the rain forest on the Pacific coast. It once consisted of vast stands of immense trees, and gave the impression of endlessness. That impression was mistaken.

Urban, industrial, and agricultural sprawl in southern Ontario have reduced this once extensive biological community to but a few precious remnants. Several pockets are preserved in national and provincial parks, and others come under some degree of protection, public and

Autumn Leaves: On a pond in Backus Woods, leaves of the Carolinian forest pile up among dots of floating duckweed. These woods near Port Rowan, Ontario are a remnant stand of Carolinian forest.

THE EASTERN FORESTS

private. These scattered pieces contain plants and animals that occur nowhere else in Canada.

Stands of hardwoods in the Carolinian forest have a tropical look about them, with hanging vines and a dense, shading canopy. Many species are shade-tolerant, and young trees of every size proliferate beneath the mature ones. The illusion in spring is of a green haze, almost like being underwater. This is especially true in Rondeau Provincial Park where towering old trees are underlain by successive levels of their eventual replacements. The result is that you can't see very much, but you can hear the sharp, explosive *pit-zee* of an Acadian flycatcher, the distant, muffled drumming of a ruffed grouse, and the sudden breaking of twigs as a white-tailed deer bounds away, perhaps flashing its white flag through the curtains of greenery.

In these woodlands beech, sugar maple, and swamp oak predominate, and on the best-drained sites are found other species of oak. Basswood is also common throughout. This is the land of southern specialities, the very names of which are at odds with the typical Canadian north country image: sassafras, tulip-tree, pawpaw, Kentucky coffee-tree, sycamore, shagbark hickory, chinquapin oak, and many more. None of these, of course, is rare continentally, but in Canada they exist only in this warm and sheltered region of rich soils.

It follows that if there are southern plant communities, there will be southern animal communities. In these deciduous woodlands, you can occasionally see the only marsupial in Canada, the opossum. On Pelee Island in Lake Erie, there is another southerner, the fox squirrel, which although introduced, is persisting. Naturally occurring, but only in Essex County on the north shore of Lake Erie, is the eastern mole, common and widespread in the United States, but having only this single outpost in Canada. Taking advantage of the tunnels of these and other moles is the woodland vole, strictly confined in Canada to a narrow band along Lake Erie. Since the presence of such small mammals invites the attention of foxes, the lithe, beautiful, and sometimes tree-climbing grey fox occurs here in modest numbers.

It is the birds, however, that attract the greatest number of naturalists to the Carolinian forest. In Canada several southern songbirds can be seen only here. One of the most noteworthy is the prothonotary warbler, known to many as the golden swamp warbler. This brilliant-coloured little bird nests in the shade of heavily wooded, well-watered swamps, usually in stumps or fallen trees. Since it prefers a low site near the water surface, the glow of its comings and goings is reflected in dark, shaded pools. The effect is almost unreal, as though the light source were too bright to be natural. Away from the water, in the thickest understorey

of the hardwoods, are hooded and Kentucky warblers. In brushy thickets are blue-winged and golden-winged warblers. Emanating from the densest vegetation above are the excruciatingly thin, ever-so-slightly peevish notes of the blue-grey gnatcatcher. These birds are difficult to see; all are skulkers that refuse to abandon the security of their visually impenetrable retreats for more than a few seconds.

Although the presence of so many birds typical of the deep south is sufficient reason for the fame of Ontario's Carolinian forest, the region possesses another extraordinary distinction: it is one of the finest places on the continent to observe bird migration. Especially noteworthy are two sand and gravel spits jutting into Lake Erie from its northern shore — Point Pelee and Long Point. Both are world famous.

Most land birds don't like to cross open water. They prefer to hug shorelines that lie in the general direction of flight. Since the orientation of Lake Erie is northeast-southwest, enormous flows of migrants proceed along its edges. Also fingers of land jutting into the lake are excellent arrival and take-off points, if flying across the lake simply cannot be avoided. Thus at both Point Pelee and Long Point, there are often enormous concentrations of birds, coming and going, feeding, or simply milling about awaiting appropriate signals from the winds. Birdwatchers can count on seeing at least 100 species in a single day at either of these places at the peak of spring migration.

The fall migration of songbirds along Lake Erie is also impressive, though not the equal of spring. At this time, much excitement derives from the migration of monarch butterflies and of certain dragonflies. Masses of the butterflies have been moving slowly southwest along the shores of Lake Ontario and Erie, eventually to the tip of Point Pelee. Here, great numbers rest for the night in stands of red cedars. Some evenings individual trees are plastered with hundreds, perhaps thousands, of orange butterflies. In the morning after the dew has dried from their wings, they take off over the lake toward Texas, California, and Mexico.

Virtually every species of eastern North American hawk can be seen along Lake Erie in the fall, but the most spectacular flights are those of broad-winged and sharp-shinned hawks. The broad-wings are buteos, or soaring hawks, and even though they may move at very great heights, they still follow the lakeshore, coasting along where lake bluffs and hillsides promote upward air movements. The sharp-shins are accipiters, or bird hawks. They tend to remain much closer to the ground, alternately flapping and sailing. Occasionally they move in very large numbers into Point Pelee, funnelling toward the tip of the peninsula before venturing out over the water.

No account of this area would be complete without mention of its reptiles. Indeed this region, exemplified at Long Point and Rondeau Provincial Park, is refuge for a number of species found nowhere else in Canada and for others which have become increasingly rare in southern Ontario. Perhaps the most arresting of these is the water-loving fox snake, a large species for which the record length is 174 centimetres. Blotched and reddish brown, it is sometimes mistaken for a venomous copperhead, which does not occur in Canada. It may vibrate its tail when frightened, whereupon it is misidentified as a rattlesnake, which is not found in this region. For these reasons the handsome fox snake is often killed, even though it is completely harmless.

Long Point: Projecting into Lake Erie, this peninsula is bordered by extensive marshes which attract a rich variety of wildlife. Long Point is an important staging area for migrating birds, bats, monarch butterflies, and dragonflies, and is home for a number of rare reptiles.

163

Bulrush and Swamp Sparrow:
Carrying an insect to its young, a
swamp sparrow pauses on a bulrush
in the marshes of Long Point. One of
the most conspicuous plants of
wetlands, bulrush is found across
Canada. The seeds are eaten by
ducks and shorebirds, and the stems
and rootstocks are food for geese
and muskrats. Stands of bulrush are
important cover for many kinds of
birds and animals. When a marsh is
drained the large animals that it
supported must find another source
of food and shelter, or die. Wetlands
are fast disappearing and those
that remain may well be at
capacity already.

Broad-winged Hawks: At her
nest in the leafy forest canopy, a
broad-winged hawk feeds chunks of
a small rodent to her young. This
crow-sized, soaring hawk can travel
almost effortlessly by riding on
currents of rising air. During
migration broad-wings travel along
ridges and lakeshores where the air
is deflected upward, enabling the
birds to cover scores of kilometres
with scarcely a flap. In autumn near
Port Stanley on the north shore of
Lake Erie, 70,000 broad-winged
hawks have been seen in a single
day, sailing high overhead toward the
south.

Snapping Turtle: Straining against hard packed sand and gravel, a snapping turtle uses its hind legs to claw out a hole into which 25 to 50 round, soft-shelled eggs will be laid. They will be covered up by the turtle and may hatch out in 10 weeks, or sometimes not until the following spring. Adaptable to a wide variety of aquatic habitats, snapping turtles are common throughout most of the eastern forest region and in southern Manitoba and Saskatchewan. They eat almost anything dead or alive including aquatic plants, marsh birds, fish, and small mammals.

Sugar Maples: In Gatineau Park near Ottawa, sugar maples show their famous autumn colours. The sugar maple is a climax species, meaning that its saplings grow readily in the shade, allowing stands of this tree to reproduce indefinitely in a stable environment. The maple is one of Canada's most valuable trees, not only to humans as a colourful tourist attraction and source of syrup and lumber, but also to many animals. Most parts of the tree — flowers, seeds, buds, twigs, foliage, and bark — are eaten by wildlife.

The most seriously threatened fauna in the Carolinian forest are likely the turtles. The systematic draining of wetlands in Ontario, as virtually everywhere in southern Canada, has grievously reduced habitat for several turtle species, especially the map, Blanding's, wood, spotted, and spiny softshell. Preservation of habitat of these and other fresh water reptiles (and amphibians) is one of the most critical environmental challenges of our time.

GREAT LAKES-ST. LAWRENCE FOREST

The Great Lakes-St. Lawrence forest extends from the edge of the Carolinian forest in southern Ontario, north to Lake Superior, and east to the Gulf of St. Lawrence. In spite of its large size, it is essentially a transitional area between the broadleaved forests of the Carolinian region and the vast, coniferous boreal forests of the north. Its transitional nature is so gradual and penetrates so deeply into the whole region that there is little or no distinctive core. It is best described as mixed.

168

The key to the mixture is conifers, which are only thinly distributed in the south but become increasingly common as we move northward. Of these the most visible are red and white pines and eastern hemlock. The latter usually grows in association with beech and sugar maple.

To the north signs of the boreal forest become visible at about the latitude of Algonquin Park, where there are still beech, maple, and hemlock, but where you begin to find spruce, white birch, balsam fir, and jack pine. This mingling of communities continues eastward until red spruce becomes conspicuous, signalling the proximity of the Acadian forest of the Maritimes.

The Great Lakes-St. Lawrence forest encompasses the area of greatest human concentration in Canada, including as it does industrialized southern Ontario and Quebec. For this reason, samples of the original conditions that prevailed are almost impossible to find. Even those areas now within the parks systems were heavily logged and burned at various times before they achieved protected status.

These forests then are representative of various stages of "succession" leading back to the original forest type which the land and climate naturally supported before European settlement. The result is a mosaic over the entire region, with plots of different sizes in earlier or later stages of regeneration, the very patchiness of which is the naturalist's greatest treasure: variety and diversity. The list of bird species in this region, for example, is the greatest in Canada, rivalled only by the extreme southern part of British Columbia.

The effect of human settlement, industry, and agriculture on the eastern forests has greatly increased some types and ages of forests at the expense of others. As a result there are certain wildlife species today that are more abundant than in earlier times

Summer Meadow: This field near Perth, Ontario is overgrown with Queen Anne's lace, goldenrod, and purple loosestrife. In the absence of the original forest, such roadside meadows provide better habitat for wildlife than a field of cultivated crops or residential backyards. They offer seclusion and brushy cover for nesting songbirds, pheasants, quail, and even some waterfowl species. Perhaps most important, these untended fields provide refuge for a variety of insects that pesticides have eliminated from cultivated areas, acting as a gene bank for life forms that may someday thrive again. Introduced plant species, such as purple loosestrife, often take over lands cleared of forests, crowding out the native vegetation that is more useful to wildlife.

169

White-tailed Deer: The most common large animal of the eastern forests zone, the white-tailed deer is best known for its foot-long tail. Many authorities believe that when a deer's tail goes up it is to signal a predator and not to warn other deer. This theory is derived from observations that the tail signal is directed not toward nearby deer but toward the perceived danger. As most predators are slower than the white-tail and rely on surprise attack, the raised tail tells them they have been discovered and that pursuit will likely be unsuccessful. The advantage for deer is that they save the energy of protracted flight.

and others whose numbers have fallen. This phenomenon is illustrated by the white-tailed deer. You will see few deer in a mature forest of hemlock, considered by some as the climax forest in the northern parts of this region. For one thing, deer cannot eat hemlock. For another, deer are animals of forest openings and early successional stages, browsing on young deciduous twigs. In the days before human settlement, there would likely have been deer where there had been fire, or perhaps tornadoes, but in few other places. In fact, deer must have been fairly uncommon in pre-pioneer days over most of the region. Today, as a result of logging activity, they are abundant.

Similarly, in earlier times there were fewer black bears. They fed on blueberries and raspberries in areas cleared by fire, flood, or storms. Today there is much more of that kind of habitat and consequently more bears. A definite beneficiary of human settlement has been the little house wren, a bird that was scarce in the days before the forest was broken up, and is very numerous today. Another is the cardinal, which dislikes dense woods. In contrast, the eastern bluebird has suffered due to loss of breeding habitat and usurpation of nest sites by introduced European starlings.

All this, of course, should not be interpreted as a rationalization for the urban-industrial blight that is in the process of permanently disfiguring the face of Canada. Rather it shows that within limits, there are species of plants and animals able to take advantage of change, whether sudden or gradual, and that the various intermediate stages of forest recovery are richer in animal species than fully mature stands. The important thing is that natural regeneration be allowed to continue. Stalled, nature can no longer produce the changing diversity of life forms that is the essence of natural process.

With the exception of a small outpost in extreme western Ontario and southern Manitoba, the distribution of the grey squirrel in Canada coincides almost exactly with the Great Lakes-St. Lawrence forest. Although it ranges throughout the eastern United States, it makes this minor intrusion into Canada where there are broadleaved deciduous trees.

The Great Lakes-St. Lawrence region remains essentially a mixture of conifers and broadleaved trees through to its eastern extremity at the Gaspé Peninsula. Along the shore of the St. Lawrence River the boreal influence is greatest with conifers predominating. Inland there are more broadleaved hardwoods, again with the familiar beech, sugar maple, and yellow birch association.

Venturing into the evergreen woods along the north shore of the St. Lawrence, you enter the habitat of the smallest mammal in the Americas, the pygmy shrew. This volatile little creature — large individuals would weigh about six grams — lives in boreal and mixed forests from Alaska to Labrador and Nova Scotia. It devours three times its own weight in food every day. Shrews must eat almost constantly and cannot afford more than the briefest rest periods, no more than one hour at a time. If they were to try to sleep the night through, they would starve to death by morning.

ACADIAN FOREST

There used to be an exhibit in the Royal Ontario Museum in Toronto of two mounted specimens — a pygmy shrew and a bull moose. On viewing the disparity in size between these two species, both warm-blooded, both furred, one could not help wonder how evolution could have produced such improbable diversity of life forms, and how such different beings could find a living in essentially the same habitat.

Part of the explanation is that they are in the same habitat only in the broadest sense. When we speak of the Acadian forest we are really lumping under one convenient title an endless list of "mini-habitats". A single tree, a single mossy puddle, a single rotting log is habitat for hundreds, perhaps thousands of species. In theory any life zone can be broken down to whatever level we wish. And evolution it seems, is willing to seize each opportunity as it arises. Once, there were elephants in these woods; now there are moose and shrews. Habitats and opportunities change with changing times.

In the eastern forests no change is quite so sudden as that caused by fire. What happens after a fire depends in great measure on what plants remain undamaged nearby. In forests such as the Acadian, chances are there will be undamaged trembling aspens in the vicinity. These and other poplars are notably opportunistic. Their seeds are light and can travel long distances quickly. But aspens need not wait for their seeds to develop, to drift away, to come to ground, to germinate, and sprout. They can spread rapidly by suckering — sending up shoots from their roots. In this way trembling aspen can cover a burn in very short order, producing an attractive small grove in the process.

Let us assume there is a small watercourse nearby. The new aspen grove in due course will be discovered by beavers. At two years of age young beavers usually leave home, striking out across country, perhaps into another watershed in search of a promising building site. Having noted a flourishing aspen food supply, they set about damming their watercourse, building a lodge, and doing all the things that beavers do, in particular creating a pond. All this industry is subsidized, as it were, by

Toppled Trees: A tangle of white cedars and yellow birch have been drowned by waters dammed by a beaver. The flooding gives the beaver easier and wider access to the forest. Floating trees and branches back to the lodge is less arduous than dragging them over land.

173

trembling aspens, themselves the immediate beneficiaries of fire.

Over time, the beavers raise successive generations of young that themselves disperse. The ponds begins to support various water-loving plants, such as pond lilies and willows, which in turn attract moose.

During the time the moose have been prospering on its plant life, the pond has been gradually shrinking. Shrubs of various kinds, grasses, sedges, mosses, and other plants have surrounded it. Siltation has begun. The beavers have long since departed. Inexorably, the combination of silting and the accumulation of plant debris shrinks the perimeter of the pond, turning it into a green meadow or sometimes a bog. The edges of northern woodland meadows and bogs are prime habitat for pygmy shrews. Together with the moose, and many plant species, they share indebtedness to beavers, to trembling aspens, and to fire.

Although natural processes remain unimpeded in some parts of the Acadian forest, most of it has been greatly influenced by human activity, especially by agriculture and forestry. This region is quite similar to the Great Lakes-St. Lawrence forest, being a transition between the boreal coniferous community of the north and the mixed hardwoods of the the south. The most visible difference is the presence of red spruce. The name of this conifer comes from the reddish brown colour of the twigs. Its needles are bright yellow-green. The more widely distributed white and black spruces grow across the boreal forest from Alaska to the Atlantic provinces. The red is strictly an easterner and southerner, being absent from the Gaspé and Newfoundland; to the west it grows a short way up the St. Lawrence River valley, disappearing around the Ottawa River. Black and white

Cattails: Perhaps the most familiar of wetland plants, cattails grow along the edges of ponds and swamps across Canada. The thick, velvety ''tail'' is a shaft packed with female flowers which are green when in bloom and brown once they have been fertilized and have developed seeds. In spring the cattail's male part, growing above the tail, is thickly covered with floppy stamens. When their pollen is released into the air, the stamens fall off leaving the characteristic cattail spike.

Crab Spider on Marsh Marigold: Camouflaged in the yellow sepals of marsh marigold, a crab spider waits to ambush an insect visiting the flower for pollen or nectar. Crab spiders do not spin webs, but hunt actively about flowers and shrubs. Males may swaddle prospective mates in silk as part of courtship.

Acadian Forest: Spruces have fallen into a stream in the Acadian forest of Nova Scotia. The presence of red spruce in these forests distinguishes them from the Great Lakes-St. Lawrence forests.

Eastern Bluebirds: Rare members of the thrush family, eastern bluebirds are not only fine singers but have brightly coloured plumage. They nest in natural tree cavities, unused woodpecker holes, or artificial nest boxes in open woodlands and orchards. Inside they build a stout nest of grass stems, bark strips, and twigs. Both sexes incubate eggs and feed the nestlings. Once the young leave the nest, the male continues to feed them while the female starts another brood. Bluebirds can rear two and sometimes three families each breeding season. The decline in bluebird numbers in recent decades was due mainly to competition with starlings and house sparrows for nesting sites, a situation that is being remedied by provision of artificial nesting boxes specially designed for bluebirds.

spruce also grow throughout the Acadian forest, the latter especially on worked-out farmland.

The Acadian forest is spruce budworm country. In spite of its name, this moth larva tends to concentrate not so much on spruce as on balsam fir, which grows nearly everywhere in the region, sometimes in pure stands, sometimes with spruce and mixed deciduous species.

Balsam fir is an extraordinarily prolific species, producing enormous numbers of seeds. When spruces have been clear-cut, almost pure stands of balsam fir take over the land thereafter. These stands, especially ones of the same age, are just what the spruce budworm larvae like best. In such areas their reproductive capacity is legendary. They fare less well in mixed coniferous-broad-leaved woodlands of varying ages. Traditional forestry practices have greatly increased opportun-

ities for the budworm by producing even-aged, single species stands, precisely the type of habitat it thrives on. Under natural conditions the spruce budworm would simply thin the forest, keep it fresh and diverse, and occasionally produce the tinder for a regenerating fire.

These forests in spring and early summer are brimming with the songs, dartings, and flutterings of several species of wood warblers, prompting the birdwatcher's greatest excitement at spring migration. These hyperactive little birds offer a brilliant array of colour and a wide variety of songs — none of which can remotely be described as a "warble". Most of them buzz, trill, or declaim more or less musically in a great diversity of tones, pitches, patterns, and forms. They also live exclusively on invertebrates, and where there are large numbers of spruce budworm moth eggs, larvae or pupae, there are usually a great many warblers.

Although the sounds of birds are everywhere in these woods, most notable are the songs of thrushes. In the southern parts of the region in damp deciduous forest, there is the descending spiral of the veery, often described as singing down a rain barrel. In both mixed and coniferous woodlands, there is the rolling musical ascent of Swainson's thrush, and the haunting, bell-like clarity of the hermit thrush.

It is well known how relatively ordinary is the plumage of some of the finest singers and how less than pleasing are the songs of many of the most flamboyantly coloured species. All this does, of course, is reveal the bias of the human eye and ear; the songs and plumages were not designed for us, but for the birds.

177

PRESERVATION

Sea Otter: This marine mammal preens much of the time, fluffing its inner fur with air to increase buoyancy and warmth. It wraps itself in the ropes and fronds of giant kelp to resist the push of incoming swells and floats on its back, scrubbing and rumpling with mitten-like forepaws. Sea otters were hunted to near extinction during the last century for their luxurious fur. Today they number about 100 in Canada, most of them reintroduced to Vancouver Island and the Queen Charlottes since 1969.

The
Status
of Nature

T he list is a terrible one. The great auk was gone in the 1840s, the Labrador duck in 1878. The sea mink was wiped out in the 1890s, almost before biologists knew it existed. The last passenger pigeon died in a zoo in 1914; before European settlement passenger pigeons numbered between three and five billion, perhaps the most numerous North American bird ever. Extirpated from Canada are the timber rattlesnake, paddle-fish, and blue walleye. A growing number of other plant and animal species face the same fate.

Although we now take nature protection for granted, the concept is barely a century old. In the aftermath of the environ-mental carnage of the 1880s, it became apparent that there were limits to exploitation after all, and that in the human interest something should be done to ensure the wise use and future productivity of nature.

At the outset, the concept was not easy to sell. The sheer abundance of North American wildlife — as exemplified by the passenger pigeon, the bison, the pronghorn, and the marine

Ferruginous Hawks: Classified as a threatened species in Canada, a ferruginous hawk steadies itself against a gust of wind with an extended wing tip. The ferruginous is very protective of its young, driving even coyotes from the nesting vicinity. Often built on the ground at the top of a canyon wall or rocky coulee, many of the large stick nests lie empty today, attesting to the decline in ferruginous numbers. Like other prairie raptors, the ferruginous hawk has suffered from a decrease in the numbers of rodents and hares, its main food, as well as from shooting and incidental poisoning by man.

mammals, as well as the apparent endlessness of the prairies, forests, lakes, and rivers — belied any notion of exhaustibility. But experience soon indicated that these assumed gifts from God were finite after all. So if people would not act in the general interest of all beings, they would be exhorted to act in their *own* interest.

The simplest way to make the point was to compare nature to a farm. Once wildlife could be seen as livestock or crops, it could be managed like any other herd of cattle or field of grain. This explains the use of the term "harvest" for the annual kill of fishes, birds, and mammals for commercial and recreational purposes. The term is also used in forestry. But how can you harvest a stand of trees you did not plant, or a shoal of fish you did not propagate, or a trophy moose you did not raise? The term harvest has become so pervasive that even wildlife protectors use it, if only to communicate with governments. The unfortunate legacy of the harvest idea is that it perpetuates and reinforces the perceived status of nature as a resource, a commodity in the human service.

The ethereal glow of a calypso orchid on the forest floor. . . the jostling clamour of a gannet colony on its cloud-shrouded Atlantic rock. . . the bubbling, twisting path of an otter under new, transparent ice. . . the conversations of a "V" of geese in a leaden autumn sky. . . Resources? Livestock? Human possessions?

Lately, though, there have been some signs of change. The establishment in 1977 of the Committee on the Status of Endangered Wildlife in Canada (COSEWIC) is one. This group of government and private biologists reviews species deemed to be in trouble, or potentially so, classifying them as rare, threatened, or endangered. The committee does not present its findings as a list of dwindling commodities, but rather as a simple accounting of imperilled beings.

This is significant. The public is expected to be interested in and, ideally, share the committee's concern. The concern is for the species themselves; it is not for how their decline might affect us.

This idea is new. Until recently concern for threatened species was limited to a small body of naturalists. Today the public is aware that many native plants and animals are in jeopardy because of human activities. And people recognize that the preservation of those species is a proper thing to work for and spend money on — not because they are resources but simply because they are in jeopardy. This is a notable step forward and it has taken place only in the last two or three decades.

Leading the way was the whooping crane. In 1941 there were 23 whooping cranes left in the world, two of them in captivity. This decline had been caused primarily by habitat loss, and by shooting during their prairie migrations and at their wintering grounds on the Gulf of Mexico. The summer breeding area, unknown until 1954, was so remote and inaccessible in Wood Buffalo National Park in northern Alberta that there was little likelihood of disturbance there.

Shortly after World War II a massive publicity campaign was mounted along the birds' migration route in the prairie provinces and states. Post offices, schools, town halls, gun clubs, newspapers, and radio stations were bombarded with posters and circulars proclaiming the crane's perilous status. Since the fall migration coincides with heavy shooting over prairie stubble fields and wetlands, gunners were entreated not to shoot at *any* large white bird, just in case. Subsequently Alberta, Saskatchewan, and Manitoba were blanketed with publicity every year from the provincial museum in Regina. Reports on the birds' numbers have appeared for 40 years in the press all over the world. That there are now almost 200 "whoopers" is testimony to the public responsiveness to an appeal that had nothing to do with the birds being a resource. People cared for the crane for its *own* sake. And thereafter, the plight of all endangered species became a matter of public awareness.

Not all endangered species are so readily embraced by the press and public. Take, for example, a chubby, dark brown, furry little animal a little bigger than a groundhog. Not a very prepossessing animal, and one that spends a good deal of time underground; this is the Vancouver Island marmot. It has no fame; it is known only to biologists and to a small group of volunteers dedicated to its interests. But it has a claim upon all of us because there may be even fewer Vancouver Island marmots than there are whooping cranes. The marmot's survival hinges largely on pre-servation of its habitat. Because it is such a slow breeder, it will take many years for the few remaining colonies to rebuild their numbers.

Slow reproduction is one of the most important limitations on many species of animals and plants —from giant coastal conifers to delicate lady's slipper orchids. Even given absolute protection, it may take a very long time to renew populations.

As this is written, the Vancouver Island marmot and the whooping crane are both on the endangered list, meaning that their "existence in Canada is threat-ened with immediate extirpation or extinction through-out all or a significant portion of their range, owing to the actions of man". Seven mammals, eight birds, three fishes, one reptile and fifteen plants are classified as endangered species by COSEWIC. Another group of animals and plants is described as "threatened", meaning that they are "likely to become endangered in Canada if the factors affecting vulnerability do not become reversed". This group includes five mammals, six birds, six fishes, and thirteen plants.

There has been some success in inducing threat-ened and endangered species to breed in captivity, but

Humpback Whale and Gull:
The humpback whale is a favourite of whale-watchers because of its varied surface acrobatics, its haunting solo songs lasting up to 30 minutes, and its curiosity and friendliness towards people. During the last century the humpback was hunted to near extinction. Although it has been protected by international agreement since 1966, it is still rare on both coasts, with less than 10 percent of its original population surviving.

somewhat less in the release of their offspring to the wild. Of course if the natural habitat is gone, the progeny born as a result of the breeding program have nowhere to go. Artificial insemination is being used more and more, particularly with peregrine falcons, which had been decimated by the widespread use of pesticides, especially DDT. Successful releases of peregrines have been going on for a number of years.

One of the more interesting breeding programs involves the swift fox. The smallest of the four foxes in Canada, it is little bigger than a house cat. Earth-coloured and slender, it is a native of the arid flatland of the southern prairies. Driven completely out of Canada half a century ago by the advance of agriculture, a few individuals survived in the United States where there was a great deal more of the kind of arid habitat that is to their liking.

To reintroduce the swift fox to Canada, a breeding project was begun in Alberta in 1973 with animals imported from the south. The first releases to the wild were made 10 years later, and by the end of 1987, 80 animals had been released and a few had bred after being set free. While the long term success of the effort cannot yet be predicted, what is clear is that the imaginative effort and dedication of modern wildlife workers are at dramatic odds with those of the early settlers.

The homesteading, settlement, and commercial farming attack on prairie wildlife in the early 1900s was perhaps the most singleminded and relentless campaign of animal extermination Canada has experienced. Dr. Wayne Lynch describes the onslaught as the first explorers were followed by the settlers: "They poured into the Prairies, secure in the belief that the land was theirs. The conquest was rapid as they poisoned, trapped, and plowed away the native creatures. Within 30 years, the plains grizzly was gone and so were most of the wolves and bison. When

the large animals had disappeared, smaller animals became targets. Coyotes, ground squirrels, and prairie dogs were irritants to be eliminated with poisons and traps. There were many innocent victims."

Prairie wildlife used to be considered as competing for the land with human interests. They were vermin to be hunted, poisoned, driven out. The story was only slightly different on the Atlantic coast. There, it was not a matter of competition; it was sheer commercial greed. The Atlantic grey whale and the St. Lawrence population of the Atlantic walrus were eliminated before 1750. The beluga (white) whales of the St. Lawrence River are now considered endangered, as well as the right whale. The Atlantic humpback is listed as rare (the Pacific humpback is threatened). What is not yet extinct is the 19th century exploitation mentality: witness the years of waffling by federal and provincial governments concerning the clubbing of newborn harp seals.

Efforts to save the great whales were late in coming but they have come, and are widely publicized and supported. Once considered as nothing more than unfeeling blocks of oily blubber free for the taking, these mysterious and compelling giants have come to occupy a very special, even mystical, place in our lives. Success stories are beginning to be told, such as the dramatic recovery of the Pacific grey whales in response to protection. Grey whale-watching lookouts are located along the west coast from British Columbia to Baja California. In fact, whale-watching has become an increasingly popular tourist attraction on both coasts.

Today's interest in the whales may well become an historical watershed in wildlife preservation. The slaughter of whales began centuries ago and has continued in our own time, remnant populations of most species surviving today only because they became too few to be worth pursuing — it's called

188

commercial extinction. A few years ago, though, something happened.

Frustrated by the failure of international diplomacy through the International Whaling Commission, an organization calling itself "Greenpeace" decided it was time to replace blathering with action. By one courageous act they brought the plight of the whales to world attention. A small group of protestors managed to manoeuvre a tiny open boat directly into the path of a Soviet whaling vessel at the moment of its attack on a whale. Undeterred, the whaler fired its harpoon, which sailed over the little boat and the heads of its occupants. That one brief moment, recorded on film, was seen wherever there were television sets. It had a single, unequivocal message: there are people who care.

As it turned out, there were a great many people who cared. Volunteer whale protection groups blossomed the world over. The plight of the whales captured our hearts, and the animals themselves captured our imaginations. Today, whales symbolize the nature preservation movement as no creatures ever have before. Whales, dolphins, and porpoises have become special. Most of us rarely see them, but it warms and inspires us just to know they are there, there in the unfathomable depths, thinking, knowing, singing, communicating, observing. . . forgiving.

Protection efforts have come late to fresh water communities, the wetlands of the country. The term "wetlands" includes ponds and marshes, swamps, fens, and bogs. The three prairie provinces contain 37 percent of all of Canada's wetlands; in the south they take the form of sloughs, potholes, lakes, and marshes; in the north, boreal lakes and bogs. On the southern grasslands, about 40,000 hectares a year are being drained in the name of "land improvement", or "land reclamation". This has made life extremely difficult not only for ducks such as mallards and

Eared Grebe: Atop a floating nest in a slough near Calgary, an eared grebe incubates a clutch of eggs. Totally aquatic, grebes are dependent on wetlands for survival. As marshes and sloughs are drained to provide land for agriculture or urban development, it becomes more difficult for wetland plants and animals to sustain viable population levels.

Red Eft: An aquatic salamander, the red-spotted newt passes through a land-dwelling stage for two to three years; during this time it is commonly called a red eft. After the eft stage, the newt darkens in colour, adapts its shape to an aquatic habitat, and returns to the water to breed. Unlike birds which can fly, amphibians and reptiles are unable to move far to find new habitat should theirs be damaged or destroyed.

Point Pelee: A turkey vulture rides the thermals over Point Pelee. Known for its Carolinian forest, its migrations of birds and butterflies, and its rare reptiles, Point Pelee is one of Canada's smallest national parks. Unfortunately, it is cut off from other natural areas by farmland and urban development. The isolation of such wild pockets increases their vulnerability to pollution, epidemic disease, and other natural disasters and limits genetic change and adaptability of plants and animals.

canvasbacks, but for the entire prairie wetland community, from midges to muskrats, from dragonflies to duckweed.

A major difficulty for nature preservation in the settled parts of Canada is fragmentation of habitat. There may remain a modest amount of Carolinian wetland in Ontario, or of the Garry oak/arbutus community in southern British Columbia, or small pieces of dryland prairie — but all are isolated and separated by paved, planted, plowed, pastured, and built-upon land. This blocks the flow of both animals and plants between the individual pockets. The result is that fresh new genetic potential is precluded. Also, such small areas put severe limitations on the number of birds that can nest.

But at least birds can fly. The sedentary creatures, such as reptiles and amphibians, are pretty well stuck where they are. When they do move they need protective cover; without it they are doomed. And for them the dangers of isolation in too small an area are becoming more critical all the time. Many plants are similarly pinned down. Species with light seeds, such as grasses, most of the daisies, and some conifers, can travel widely on the wind. Heavy-fruited nut trees, though, rely on some animal to transport their seeds. When there are no natural corridors between remaining stands of many of the hardwoods, seed dispersal is shut down. Moreover, there appears to be a critical size below which a community cannot survive. The combination of diminishing size, fragmentation, and resulting isolation of communities may well be the gravest nature preservation problem of our time.

Unfortunately for nature, Canada has evolved with a resource extraction bias, one that is still quite apparent in political affairs. This is why so many people still refer to moose, tundra swans, beluga whales, and Douglas-firs as resources. Founded as we were on the skins of mammals, built as we were on

White Pelican: A tiny, naked pelican chick sits beneath its mother's protective body. White pelicans nest in island colonies on lakes where they are safe from predatory mammals and human disturbance. The white pelican, once a threatened species in Canada, has recovered its numbers during the last 10 years.

trees, fishes, minerals, and topsoils, this is scarcely surprising.

Ours is the species that treats the land as though it owned it. No other animal does this. Granted many species declare and defend their personal spaces, but this has nothing to do with ownership; it has everything do with participation in their communities, each in its physical and social place. But place means a great deal more than habitat. For wild nature to continue today, it needs a place in the human consciousness. Once we give it that place, preservationists will be working not on behalf of nature or its usefulness to us, but to sustain nature as an integral part of our being. There are some good signs.

In 1987, for the first time ever, a species was *removed* from the endangered list in Canada. Because of human encroachment on its nesting islands in the prairie provinces, the white pelican was thought to be headed toward oblivion. Conspicuous in dazzling white, with a wingspread up to three metres, and breeding in colonies on accessible lakes, the pelican seemed made to order for annihilation. But it didn't happen. Under careful protection, the birds showed that given a reasonable chance they can take care of themselves.

That is only part of the good news. The pelicans have shown us more than their survival potential. Their story indicates that a century after the desecration of nature reached its peak in Canada, a new human consciousness has begun to emerge. The change is very slow, but treasured beliefs and assumptions always die hard. As in all evolutionary processes, however, death brings new life, and new life means new beings with new eyes, new sensibilities, new feelings.

We watch the pelicans gliding stiff-winged, gleaming white, across the prairie sky. The majestic procession is an event, an experience in which we are no longer mere observers, but active participants. We take these magnificent creations deep into our being and a new reality is born within us. There has been a change of status for the pelicans . . . and for us.

193

Western Sandpipers: During migration large numbers of sandpipers may be observed at locations along both coasts. In Boundary Bay near Vancouver, western sandpipers, in flocks of a thousand or more, flash their white bellies and dark backs in synchronised aerial displays called "helioscoping". These manoeuvres are thought to confuse falcons and hawks which prey on them.

1. *High Arctic Wildlife.* Muskoxen, polar bears, wolves, arctic hares at Polar Bear Pass. Bathurst Island. Summer.
2. *Caribou Migration.* Large herds cross Dempster Highway north of Dawson City. Fall.
3. *Coastal Grizzly Bears.* Prime habitat at Khutzeymateen Estuary north of Prince Rupert. August.
4. *Killer Whales.* Whale rubbing beaches at Robson Bight in Johnstone Strait, Vancouver Island. Summer.
5. *West Coast Wildlife.* Sea otters, sea lions, grey whales. Pacific Rim National Park. Spring, summer.
6. *Tall Trees.* Largest trees in Canada. Nimpkish Valley and Cathedral Grove.
7. *Vancouver Island Marmots:* Colonies of endangered marmots on Green Mountain near Nanaimo.
8. *Spring Wildflowers.* Abundant woodland species. Vancouver Island and the Gulf Islands. April-May.
9. *Birds of Prey.* Bald eagles, snowy owls, gyrfalcons, many others at Boundary Bay. Winter.
10. *Adam's River Sockeye Run.* Peak runs every four years near Kamloops. Fall.
11. *Pocket Desert.* Cacti, rattlesnakes, kangaroo rats near Osoyoos. June.
12. *Alpine Wildflowers.* Meadows accessible by car at Mount Revelstoke National Park. Summer.
13. *Mountain Wildlife.* Bighorn sheep, elk, mountain goats, black bears in Banff, Jasper, and Kananaskis parks. Summer.
14. *Waterfowl and Shorebirds.* Concentrations of migrants at Beaverhill Lake. Spring, fall.
15. *Prairie Wildlife.* Pronghorns, ferruginous hawks, coyotes, rattlesnakes. Milk River region, May-June.
16. *Endangered Whooping Cranes.* Also white pelicans, sandhill cranes at Last Mountain Lake. Late August, early September.
17. *Arctic Wildlife.* Polar bears, beluga whales, arctic foxes at Churchill. Fall.
18. *Rare Orchids.* Bruce Peninsula National Park. Spring, summer.
19. *Bird and Butterfly Migrations.* Point Pelee and Long Point. Spring, fall.
20. *Backus Woods.* Pocket of Carolinian forest near Port Rowan.
21. *Snow Geese Staging Area.* Large concentrations at Cap-Tourmente. Fall.
22. *St. Lawrence River Whales.* Endangered beluga whales, also fin, humpback, blue, minke near Tadoussac. Summer.
23. *Northern Gannets.* World's second largest colony. Bonaventure Island. June-July.
24. *Tantramar Marshes.* Prime habitat for breeding birds and migrants, north of Sackville. Spring, fall, winter.
25. *Atlantic Seabird Rookeries.* Northern gannets, black kittiwakes, common murres at Cape St. Mary's. June-July.

SPECIAL FLORA AND FAUNA MAP GUIDE

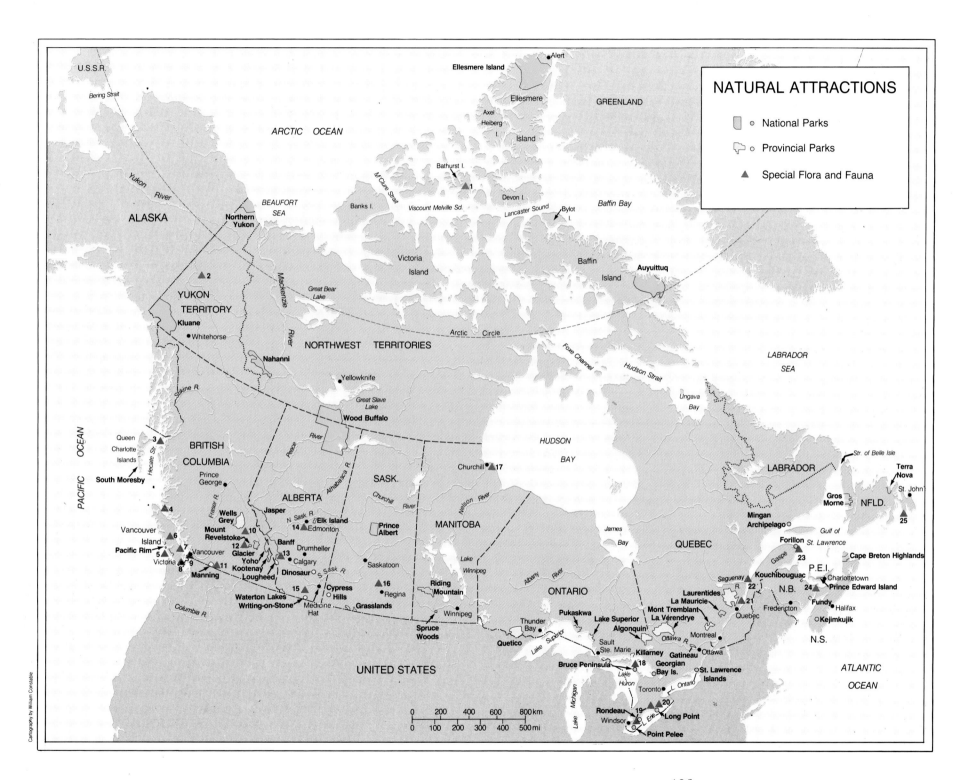

NATURAL ATTRACTIONS

☐ ○ National Parks

▽ ○ Provincial Parks

▲ Special Flora and Fauna

Selected References

Allen, Robert Thomas. 1970. *The Great Lakes.* Toronto: Natural Science of Canada Limited.

Banfield, A.W.F. 1974. *The Mammals of Canada.* Toronto: University of Toronto Press.

Barry, T.W. 1968. "Observations on Natural Mortality and Native Use of Eider Ducks along the Beaufort Sea Coast." *Canadian Field-Naturalist* 82: 140-144.

Bent, Arthur Cleveland. 1946. *Life Histories of North American Jays, Crows, and Titmice.* Washington: Smithsonian Institution.

Berrill, N.J. 1951. *The Living Tide.* New York: Dodd, Mead and Company.

Biggar, H.P., ed. 1922. *The Works of Samuel de Champlain.* Toronto: The Champlain Society.

Bird, J. Brain. 1980. *The Natural Landscapes of Canada.* Toronto: John Wiley and Sons Canada Limited.

Bird, Ralph B. 1961. *Ecology of the Aspen Parkland of Western Canada.* Ottawa: Canada Department of Agriculture.

Bodsworth, Fred. 1970. *The Pacific Coast.* Toronto: Natural Science of Canada Limited.

Braithwaite, Max. 1970. *The Western Plains.* Toronto: Natural Science of Canada Limited.

Braun, E. Lucy. 1964. *Deciduous Forests of Eastern North America.* New York: Hafner Publishing Company.

Burles, Douglas, W., and Manfred Hoefs. 1984. "Winter Mortality of Dall Sheep, *Ovis dalli dalli*, in Kluane National Park, Yukon." *Canadian Field-Naturalist* 98(4): 479-484.

Calef, George. 1981. *Caribou and the Barren-lands.* Ottawa: Canadian Arctic Resources Committee.

Canada Department of Fisheries and Forestry. 1969. *Native Trees of Canada.* 7th Edition.

Clapham, W.B. Jr. 1973. *Natural Ecosystems.* New York: The Macmillan Company.

Colinveaux, Paul. 1986. *Ecology.* New York: John Wiley and Sons.

Cook, Francis, R. 1984. *Introduction to Canadian Amphibians and Reptiles.* Ottawa: National Museums of Canada.

Costello, David F. 1969. *The Prairie World.* New York: Thomas Y. Crowell Company.

Dolphin, William Ford. 1987. "Observations of Humpback Whale, *Megaptera novae-angliae* — Killer Whale, *Orcinus orca*, Interactions in Alaska: Comparisons with Terrestrial Predator-prey Relationships." *Canadian Field-Naturalist* 101(1): 70-75.

Durrell, Lee. 1986. *State of the Ark.* Garden City, N.Y.: Doubleday & Company Ltd.

Edwards, R. Yorke. 1970. *The Mountain Barrier.* Toronto: Natural Science of Canada.

Estes, James R., Ronald Tyrl, and Jere N. Brunken. 1982. *Grasses and Grasslands Systematics and Ecology.* Norman: University of Oklahoma Press.

Fitzharris, Tim. 1986. *British Columbia Wild.* Vancouver: Terrapin Press.

—. 1986. *Wildflowers of Canada.* Toronto: Oxford University Press.

Forsyth, Adrian. 1985. *Mammals of the Canadian Wild.* Camden East: Camden House Publishing Ltd.

Godfrey, W. Earl. 1986. *The Birds of Canada* (revised edition). Ottawa: National Museums of Canada.

Hardy, W.G., ed. 1967. *Alberta: A Natural History.* Edmonton: Hurtig.

Hare, F. Kenneth, and Morley K. Thomas. 1974. *Climate Canada.* Toronto: Wiley Publishers of Canada Ltd.

Harrison, Colin. 1978. *A Field Guide to the Nests, Eggs and Nestlings of North American Birds.* Glasgow: Collins.

Hunt, Charles B. 1974. *Natural Regions of the United States and Canada.* San Francisco; W.H. Freeman and Company.

Ives, Jack D., and Roger G. Barry. 1974. *Arctic and Alpine Environments.* London: Methuen.

Kelley, Don Greame. 1971. *Edge of a Continent.* Palo Alto, California: American West Publishing Company.

Kendeigh, S. Charles. 1961. *Animal Ecology.* Englewood Cliffs N.J.: Prentice-Hall Inc.

Larsen, James A. 1982. *Ecology of the Northern Lowland Bogs and Conifer Forests.* Toronto: Academic Press.

Lefolii, Ken. 1970. *The St. Lawrence Valley.* Toronto: Natural Science of Canada Limited.

Livingston, John A. 1981. *The Fallacy of Wildlife Conservation.* Toronto: McClelland and Stewart.

—. 1981. *Arctic Oil.* Toronto: Canadian Broadcasting Corporation.

—. 1970. *Canada.* Toronto: Natural Science of Canada.

Lopez, Barry. 1986. *Arctic Dreams.* New York: Charles Scribner's Sons.

—. 1978. *Of Wolves and Men.* New York: Charles Scribner's Sons.

Lowry, Lloyd F., Robert R. Nelson, and Kathryn J. Forst. 1987. "Observations of Killer Whales, *Orcinus orca*, in Western Alaska: Sightings, Strandings, and Predation on Other Marine

Mammals". *Canadian Field-Naturalist* 101(1): 6-12.

Lynch, Wayne. 1987. "The Return of the Swift Fox". *Canadian Geographic* Vol. 107 No.4.

Lyons, C.P. 1952. *Trees, Shrubs and Flowers to Know in British Columbia*. Vancouver: J.M. Dent and Sons (Canada) Limited.

Macpherson, A.G., and J. B. Macpherson, eds. 1981. *The Natural Environment of Newfoundland, Past and Present*. St. John's: Department of Geography, Memorial University of New foundland.

Mann, K.H. 1982. *Ecology of Coastal Waters: A Systems Approach*. Berkley: University of California Press.

Matsch, Charles L. 1976. *North America and the Great Ice Age*. New York: McGraw-Hill Book Company.

McCann, S.B.,ed. 1980. *The Coastline of Canada*. Ottawa: Geological Survey of Canada.

Moon, Barbara, 1970. *The Canadian Shield*. Toronto: Natural Science of Canada.

Mosquin, Theodore, and Cecile Suchal, eds. 1977. *Canada's Threatened Species and Habitats*. Ottawa: Canadian Nature Federation.

Munro, Wm. T. 1985. "Status of the Sea Otter, *Enhydra lutris*, in Canada," *Canadian Field-Naturalist* Vol. 99(3):413-416.

Myers, Norman, ed. 1984. *Gaia: An Atlas of Planet Management*. Garden City, N.Y.: Anchor Press/Doubleday & Company Ltd.

Nero, R.W., and R.W. Fyfe. 1956. "Kangaroo Rat Colonies Found." *Blue Jay* 14:107-110.

Pincus, Howard J. 1962. *Great Lakes Basin*. Washington, D.C.: American Association for the Advancement of Science.

Nettleship, David N., Timothy R.Birkhead, and Anthony J. Gaston. 1979. "Reproductive failure among Arctic Seabirds Associated with Unusual Ice Conditions in Lancaster Sound 1978". Dartmouth: Canadian Wildlife Service.

Pruitt, William O. Jr. 1978. *Boreal Ecology*. London: Edward Arnold.

Risser, P.G., E.C. Birney, H.D. Blocker, S.W. May, W.J. Parton and J.A.Wiens. 1981. *The True Prairie Ecosystem*. Stroudsburg, Pennsylvania: Hutchinson Ross Publishing Company.

Rowe, J.S. 1972. *Forest Regions of Canada*. Ottawa: Department of the Environment.

Russell, Franklin. 1970. *The Atlantic Coast*. Toronto: Natural Science of Canada.

Savage, A., and C. Savage. 1981. *Wild Mammals of Western Canada*. Saskatoon: Western Producer Prairie Books.

Smith, T.G. 1985. "Polar Bears, *Ursus maritimus*, as Predators of Belugas, *Delphinapterus leucas*," *Canadian Field-Naturalist* 99 (1): 71-75.

Stonehouse, Bernard. 1971. *Animals of the Arctic: The Ecology of the Far North*. London: Ward Lock Limited.

Taverner, P.A. 1926. *Birds of Western Canada*. Ottawa: Canada Department of Mines.

Terres, J.K. 1980. *The Audubon Society Encyclopedia of North American Birds*. New York: Alfred A. Knopf Inc.

Wilkinson, Douglas. 1970. *The Arctic Coast*. Toronto: Natural Science of Canada.

Wooding, Frederick H. 1982. *Wild Mammals of Canada*. Toronto: McGraw-Hill Ryerson Limited.

World Wildlife Fund. 1987. *Endangered Species in Canada 1987*. (Pamphlet). Toronto.

Worster, Donald. 1979. *Nature's Economy: The Roots of Ecology*. Garden City, N.Y.: Anchor Press.

Young, C. 1985. *The Forests of British Columbia*. North Vancouver: Whitecap Books.

Leopard Frog: Floating motionless in the middle of a pond, a leopard frog presents an attractive landing spot for a flying insect. Should one venture near, it risks being snagged by the frog's long, sticky tongue. Leopard frogs are found in the southern half of Canada except for British Columbia.

Acknowledgements

Tim Fitzharris I wish to thank the Royal Canadian Geographical Society for their support of this project, with particular thanks to Ross Smith, editor of *Canadian Geographic*.

It was a pleasure to work with the people at Penguin Books Canada, publisher of this book in particular Morton Mint, Catherine Yolles, and Dianne Craig.

I learned much about book production and design from Toronto book designer V. John Lee who shared his considerable knowledge and experience with me.

Special appreciation goes to Yorke Edwards, former director of the British Columbia Provincial Museum, for his critical review of the picture captions.

Thanks are extended to Erma Fitzharris, Pat and Natalie Fitzharris, and Eric and Helen Fraggalosch for their help while I was travelling in eastern Canada.

Many assisted with photographic undertakings: Tom and Lois Gilchrist made possible the photography of golden eagles on their ranch in southern Alberta. Lang Elliot and Richard and Judy Bonney helped with the photography of eastern songbirds. Laurie Henderson provided guidance on natural history attractions in the Yukon. Wayne McCrory, Peter Grant, and Vicki Husband of Friends of Ecological Reserves and Bart Robinson made possible the photography of grizzly bears at the Khutzeymateen Estuary. Andrew Bryant and Joan Robin assisted the photography of tall trees on Nimpkish Island. Kris Kahn of the Western Pacific Academy of Photography and Jerry Shulman made possible photography in Pacific Rim National Park. Mike Beedell and Gerry Ellis helped with work carried out in the Arctic. Gordy Sherman assisted with photography in the grasslands and was an inspiration for all work. Jim Fitzharris was friend and assistant on many excursions.

In particular, I wish to thank my friends Don, Cora, Noah, and Erica Li-Leger whose wide-ranging support throughout the project was invaluable.

Most important, this book could not have been completed without the help of my colleague, Audrey Fraggalosch, who carried out critical research, field work, editing and managed the entire undertaking through to publication.

John Livingston I wish to express my appreciation to Audrey Fraggalosch for her patient and constructive editing. I also wish to thank John R. Livingston for his assiduous bibliographic work.

Lake Erie Shoreline: All life grows from the basic elements of land and water and energy from the sun; and it changes constantly. The dramatic change in Canada's natural history over the past few centuries will continue, although perhaps not at the same rate.

CREATIVE PRODUCTION BY TERRAPIN PRESS, Vancouver, Canada

Managing Editor: Audrey Fraggalosch

Editor: Ross Smith

Layout: Tim Fitzharris

Cartography: William Constable

Graphic Assembly: Rod Burton, Pyramid Productions

Typography: Marcus Yearout, Digitype

Scientific Review: The National Museum of Natural Sciences, Ottawa: Dr. E. Haber, Assistant Curator, Vascular Plants Section, Botany Division; Dr. C-T. Shih, Curator, and Dr. Laubitz, Assistant Curator, Crustaceans Section, Zoology Division; Dr. F.R. Cook, Curator, Herpetology Section, Zoology Division; S.D. MacDonald, Curator, Vertebrate Ethology Section, Zoology Division, Dr. C.G. van Zyll de Jong, Curator, Mammalogy Section, Zoology Division; and Dr. C.R. Harington, Curator, Quaternary Zoology Section, Paleobiology Division.